Compliments Of:

OEHME, VAN SWEDEN & ASSOCIATES, INC.

GARDENS BY WOLFGANG OEHME AND JAMES VAN SWEDEN

The New
American
Garden

The New

American

Garden

CAROLE OTTESEN

MACMILLAN PUBLISHING COMPANY
New York
COLLIER MACMILLAN PUBLISHERS
London

Opulent ground cover edges a
path in a lush but tiny garden
in New Orleans's densely
populated French Quarter.

Macmillan Publishing Company
866 Third Avenue, New York, N.Y. 10022
Collier Macmillan Canada, Inc.

Library of Congress Cataloging-in-Publication Data

Ottesen, Carole, 1942–   The New American garden.

Bibliography: p.   Includes index.
1. Gardens, American.   2. Landscape gardening—United States.   I. Title.
SB457.53.O88   1987   712'.6'0973   87-7797

ISBN 0-02-594090-2

Macmillan books are available at special discounts for bulk purchases
for sales promotions, premiums, fund-raising, or educational use.
For details, contact:

Special Sales Director
Macmillan Publishing Company
866 Third Avenue
New York, N.Y. 10022

10 9 8 7 6 5 4 3 2 1

Printed in the United States of America

Contents

Acknowledgments

TO THOSE CLEAR-EYED GARDENERS of the past, Wilhelm Miller and Jens Jensen, who indicated a new direction and to present day gardeners all across the country who offered food, drink, and good company in addition to splendid examples of new American gardens: profound thanks! Special thanks to Norm Hooven of Limerock Ornamental Grasses for answering many questions about grasses, and to Wolfgang Oehme and Jim van Sweden for their generous good will.

The New
American
Garden

The Garden as Landscape The Landscape as Garden

I T   I S   T I M E for a new American garden. For two hundred years Americans have installed modified versions of the English landscaped park around their homes and places of business. This style of landscaping was all the rage—in 1776. Colonial Americans consciously copied English style, but those who followed mindlessly copied those who went before, eventually establishing a rigid conformity to lawn and shrubbery that ignored the unique flora, fauna, and climates of the American continent.

Now, gardening on this side of the Atlantic is coming into its own with a style that is fresh and new—and distinctly American. Emerging all over the country, American-style gardens brim with soft, full, re-laxed—often wild—plantings that complement the local landscape, adapt to regional growing conditions, and respond to seasonal change. These are gardens that express themselves in the vernacular, often using native plants and drawing inspiration from the natural setting, rather than from conventional gardening models. They are nostalgic gardens, re-storing the unique flora of a new land.

This new look is the product of a coming together of the separate disciplines of gardening and landscaping, coupled with a sophisticated grasp of gardening dynamics and a concern for native plants and wild-life. For too long "landscaping" automatically meant a reflex installation of lawn and exotic evergreen shrubs, and "gardening" meant growing

Lawn used to be considered indispensable even in the Southwest where rainfall is seasonal. Now, a new con-cept, xeriscaping—low-water-use landscaping—not only saves time, money, and re-sources but blends beautifully into the natural surroundings. Plantings adjacent to a walk-way of Mexican tile leading to an Arizona house include ground cover of salvia and In-dian fig accented by a tall, sculptural ocotillo, *Fouquieria splendens*. Red blooming bou-gainvillea softens the wall. *(Photo and design by Steve Martino & Associates)*

flowers, vegetables, and everything else in special beds. "Landscaping" was the correct public face of a property. And people held definite notions about which plants were suitable landscape plants and which were not. Most often, the landscaping used in front of a house was static green—a "foundation planting" consisting of a string of woody evergreens, such as boxwood, hollies, or junipers, lined up in front of the house. This custom is a leftover from the days when houses had unsightly foundations that needed covering.

The average house was landscaped so that its lawn and foundation planting were visible from the street—but not from within the house. What was gained by conforming to the commonly held notion of landscaping was lost, however, in beauty and enjoyment as seen from within.

While landscaping dominated the public side of a property, gardening, with the exception of a few bulbs or annuals, was hidden from public view—done in the privacy of the backyard, often in long, narrow beds bordering the lawn. Because of the ephemeral nature of herbaceous plants, flower gardening was considered "messy" and had to be done only in prescribed places—generally, out of the public eye.

Necessary accoutrements of a respectable property included foundation planting and lawn—the more highly manipulated, the better. Lawn was considered indispensable. A homeowner would move boulders, cut down trees, fight grubs, then lime, fertilize, water, aerate, and mow and mow and mow to have it. No matter what the natural landscape around his house looked like—even if it were desert, he would have his lawn—regardless of the cost in time, effort, and water.

This long and needless enslavement of the American homeowner to his lawn mower is finally ending. Going, too, are the deliberately isolated flower border, the practice of pruning hedges, and the necessity for a garage full of pesticides. Conformity to static green American versions of English landscape is finally passing on. Here to stay is a dynamic new garden. Exciting, nostalgic, romantic, environmentally sensitive, the new garden is, nevertheless, quintessentially American in its easy-care good looks.

Landscaping and gardening have merged into a total garden encompassing an entire property rather than just an isolated flower bed or border. Masses of what were once considered exclusively garden plants are turning up as exquisite ground cover in exciting and innovative landscaping. Small, geometric beds are disappearing as their erstwhile occupants join in bold masses that flow over the ground, conforming to contours of the land and differentiating along patterns of light and shade. Instead of a series of different-use areas—lawn, vegetable and flower beds, paths, outdoor living area—the new American garden features functional paved areas with flowing interlocking masses of native plants or flowering garden subjects on a scale effective in the landscape. Massed ground cover of beautiful and very sturdy plants softens sophisticated,

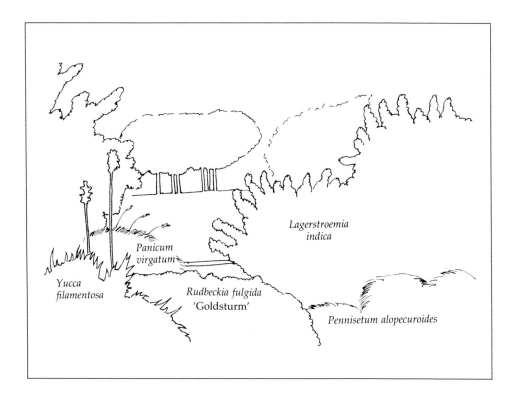

Yucca
filamentosa

Panicum
virgatum

Rudbeckia fulgida
'Goldsturm'

Lagerstroemia
indica

Pennisetum alopecuroides

Gardening and landscaping are coming together in a new American garden. Instead of static, funereal evergreens, masses of dynamic perennials—*Rudbeckia fulgida* 'Goldsturm,' fountain grass *(Pennisetum alopecuroides),* and switch grass *(Panicum virgatum)*—turn the entire landscape into a garden at Pershing Park in Washington, D.C. Seasonal changes keep the landscaping dynamic. After the rudbeckias bloom, hundreds of dark chocolate-brown seed heads form on the plants, constituting a second, more subdued show. Grasses, which blanch to shades of almond after frost, evergreen *Yucca filamentosa,* and the sinewy trunks of pink-blooming crape myrtles provide winter interest. *(Design by Oehme, van Sweden & Associates)*

practical, no-nonsense American design to accommodate parking, circulation, and outdoor living spaces. Statuesque plants with magnetic presence serve as living sculpture, while carefully selected combinations provide year-round interest. Plants in the new garden not only look right in their settings but require only minimal upkeep because they are biologically suited to their microclimates.

Like all revolutions, this one has come to fruition for a variety of reasons. Profound changes in the American life-style—shrinking property sizes, increasing water and fuel costs and shortages, and both adults of many households working outside the home—are playing a role. Boredom with traditional green landscaping that is outdated and unsuited to the climate is one factor. Life-styles that leave no time or enthusiasm for a weekend of clipping and mowing is another. Most important, in the wake of a great wave of gardening interest, Americans have educated themselves to be sophisticated, knowledgeable gardeners. Traditionally "correct" landscaping—neither intellectually satisfying nor labor-effective—no longer satisfies. Fortified with knowledgeable concern for wildlife and the environment and a connoisseur's delight in both native and exotic perennial plants, the American gardener confidently turns away from models of the past to create a uniquely American style: beautiful, sensible, functional, and fuss-free.

In spite of diminishing space for gardens and a shortage of time and resources both natural and otherwise to maintain them, Americans are demanding more from their gardens, not less. The longing for random and untrammeled nature grows in direct correlation to the increasingly urban environment in which most people live and garden. Even the tiniest property must provide an outdoor living space surrounded by all the mystery, excitement, and beauty that is conveyed in the word "garden." It must contain a valid extension of the living space, a special transitional place halfway between inside and out that is a retreat from the harshness and noise of the outside world. This outdoor room must be enfolded, protected, surrounded, and hidden by layers of luxuriant vegetation.

In spite of obstacles such as limited space and resources, Americans are constructing gardens of haunting beauty whose upkeep is managed easily. They are providing spaces for man in nature where fleeting wild flowers—and wildlife—appear and disappear alongside outdoor living areas. They are creating urban oases, places of movement and excitement that allow for tremendous seasonal changes in mass and density. They are recapturing the spirit of the frontier with meadow and prairie gardens covered by sweeps of herbaceous perennials and ornamental grasses. They are gardening in the West and Southwest with native plants suited to climate. Finally, American gardeners are allowing gardens to be spontaneous, to change and move toward a delicate and unique balance of plant life.

The influence of England, long the arbiter of gardening taste, has

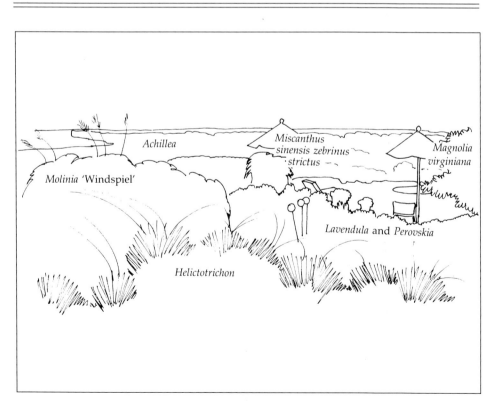

No longer confined to geometric beds and borders, perennials and ornamental grasses landscape a waterfront house on New York's Long Island with magnificent ground cover. Massed garden plants, blue oat grass (*Helictotrichon sempervirens*), tall purple moor grass (*Molinia caerulea altissima* 'Windspiel'), Russian sage (*Perovskia atriplicifolia*), lavender, and achillea around an outdoor living space combine in a low, windbreaking, no-mow meadow that blends into the surrounding landscape.

Luxuriant vegetation transforms a tiny New Orleans, Louisiana, backyard into a green oasis for wildlife and people. In the heart of the densely populated French Quarter, this tiny garden's central fish pool is nearly hidden by a delightfully eclectic collection of edible and ornamental plants.

been supplanted by respect for the home country, with regional models better suited to American climatic zones and life-style. Many of the plants traditionally associated with an English-style perennial border or cottage garden are still in use, but the way in which they are used is completely new. No longer relegated to residential flower borders, these plants mix with sturdy natives as magnificent ground cover. Composed of masses of flowers, clumps of grasses, perennials, meadows, prairies, and desert flora, exciting new ground cover is springing up unexpectedly in front of houses, banks, and office buildings. Wild flowers—not lawn—are blooming along American highways. Prairie surrounds corporate offices, replacing the lackluster old-style lawn and foundation planting.

Practical as well as beautiful, these exciting landscapes are less costly than their lawn and evergreen counterparts—to the environment and pocketbook, and in hours of upkeep. Matching plants and garden sites by cultural zone allows for healthier plants and lower maintenance. In addition, the concept of xeriscaping—arid-region landscaping that makes only modest demands on the water supply—has arisen in the West,

When the alternative is as exciting and undemanding as this colorful meadow, the installation of lawn is no longer automatic. This meadow of wild flowers around power lines in Washington provides a long season of changing color. Wild flower mixtures are available in a variety of combinations, keyed to regional conditions.
(Photo courtesy of the Applewood Seed Company)

where Eastern-style landscaping not only made exorbitant demands on natural resources, but looked distinctly out of place. Trees, shrubs, and ground covers suitable to an arid region blend into the landscape, making a more harmonious whole.

A very special group of plants distinguishes the new garden. They are refreshing, exciting, and, best of all, easy to grow and care for. Sometimes they are natives, returned to these shores after years of hybridizing abroad. Sometimes they are the very plants of the wayside. Often they are exotics. In states with largely seasonal rainfall, plants from similar climates—such as Australia—beautify the landscape. The key to their success is suitability. In the hands of a knowledgeable gardener, these versatile plants produce splendid effects with only modest upkeep and minimal demands on natural resources.

When a neat, unchanging evergreen look was the unwritten rule, herbaceous perennials were excluded from consideration as landscape subjects. Only evergreen material was allowed. Now, the distinctly American concept of "easy care" combines with sophisticated design, and beautiful, sturdy, and undemanding perennials are found in the new garden. Restoring the exciting herbaceous layer of botanical life to the garden offers the rewarding challenge of including in the design dimensions of time as well as space, as groups of plants are installed to provide a sequence of bloom throughout the growing season. But evergreens—stalwart, unchanging, and utterly dependable—still have an important function in the garden. For much of the year they serve as an attractive backdrop for their mercurial cousins. Their deep, lustrous green is a perfect foil for the soft greens of new perennial growth in the early spring and the wheat and almond colors of dried grasses in the winter.

Each season brings a different face to the new garden. Spring is a rumbling of giants in the earth, with bright green tufts of grasses pushing up, croziers of ferns unfolding, and the blunt bullet heads of hostas poking up. There is a distinct sensation of change, a kind of fairy movement always slightly out of sight. Moving behind your back, still when you turn around, but always bigger, greener, more lush. After the earliest trees, witch hazel and spike winter hazel, bulbs begin their yearly show, quickly followed by the prodigious growth of the herbaceous perennials. In the West, rains signal the blooming of masses of desert plants and wild flowers. In the East, ground covers such as epimedium begin to climb the tall stalks of daffodils even before they have finished their bloom. Day by day the landscape changes as new groups of perennials emerge, forming dynamic masses. Large groups of a single type of plant lend unity and cohesion to the overall design of a garden, while interspersed sequentially blooming plant groups add spontaneity and excitement.

Summer arrives when it seems that the garden can change no more, with the grasses thick and full and the flowers covered with bloom.

By choosing "plants with the right stuff," gardeners lighten maintenance chores. Long-lived, adaptable perennials look good for most or all of the year, need little care, and perform for years. Here, low-growing *Sedum x* 'Ruby Glow' spills over a sidewalk in front of *Rudbeckia fulgida* 'Goldsturm.' The blooming grass is fountain grass (*Pennisetum alopecuroides*). Behind the mugo pine, yellow-banded porcupine grass (*Miscanthus sinensis zebrinus strictus*) contrasts brightly with evergreens.

Summer's volume of growth has totally altered the scale of the landscape. Movement slows to a languid swaying of dense clumps of grass, a flitting of birds in an otherwise drowsy, sun-drenched, bee-buzzing lushness. Growth is complete.

Transition into autumn is gradual; a gradual loss of mass, a gradual drying up and thinning out, a gradual turning of colors. The mood of the garden is one of fine melancholy. And week by week, the evergreen structure of the garden becomes more prominent.

The first frost transforms the landscape. Now earthen tones, seed pods in chocolates and rusts, and pale, frost-blanched grasses contrast with the deep luster of evergreens. Forms are spare and bony, textures dry and rustling. Winter suspends growth until the cycle begins again. In the arid West, "winter" is the dry season, when parched grasses contrast with the glaucous green aloes and agaves, mesquites and acacias.

Seasonal show rests heavily on the choice of plants—most of which are perennials. Hardworking, dependable, suited to their situations, plants in the new garden blend well. They are self-limiting in growth, have a long season of show, and adapt to local rainfall conditions. The fussy, labor-intensive practices associated with traditional perennial borders—deadheading, staking, and constantly dividing—are omitted from the garden. Dried flower heads are frequently left on the plants for late fall and winter interest. Easy to maintain, plants in the new garden are painstakingly chosen with an eye for their appearance over time.

Most gardens peak in the spring, but the new American garden is carefully planned to appeal in every season—even in the dead of winter. As seasons pass, different combinations of a series of well-chosen perennials take center stage, exhibiting subtle contrasts of foliage, stem, flower form, and color. Ornamental grasses play an important role in this new garden, working to create vast changes in scale and lasting winter interest. Wild flowers, restored to their native habitat, "naturalize" luxuriantly.

In its inclusion of grasses and native plants, the new garden evokes the American past. Sweeps of fountain grass and black-eyed Susans suggest an expanse of prairie. Cacti and succulents represent the arid West. Colonies of wild flowers recall the great woods. Replacing formal, clipped green with dynamic, changing plants is evocative of a simpler, rural life-style. Gardeners, farmers, and other country dwellers have always known and loved the hallmarks of the passing seasons: green lacy fuzz on spring trees, the golden beauty of a wheat field, strands of dried wild flowers poking seedy heads through the snow. Now this delight in the rhythmic changing of the earth's flora has become a dynamic element of American landscaping.

Herbaceous plants, both native and cultivated, are nature's dynamic subjects, returning from the dead each year to astound us with amazing growth. Emerging in spring, growing lush and full in summer, and ex-

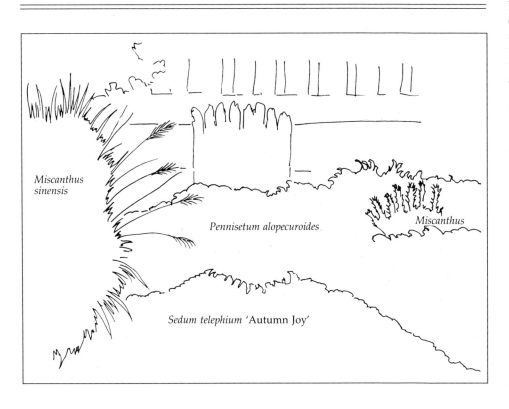

Miscanthus
sinensis

Pennisetum alopecuroides

Miscanthus

Sedum telephium 'Autumn Joy'

Dynamic landscaping of garden subjects changes with the seasons. Looking like a country field, ornamental grasses, tall Eulalia grass (*Miscanthus sinensis*) and fountain grass (*Pennisetum alopecuroides*) contrast with a mass of *Sedum telephium* 'Autumn Joy' in a stylized meadow in front of the Federal Reserve Bank Building in Washington, D.C. Grasses turn to bright shades of almond as the weather cools. 'Autumn Joy' sedum is a perennial with an amazingly long period of show. Neat, mounding, pale green plants are effective from April on. Flat flower umbels appear in summer, turning from green to pink, then darkening to brilliant red-copper in fall. In winter, dried seed stalks poke through the snow.
(Design by Oehme, van Sweden & Associates)

A burst of Atamasco lilies and sensitive ferns combine in delightful ground cover around cypress knobs in a South Carolina garden. Plants perfectly suited to setting naturalize and bring spontaneity back into the garden.

pressing melancholy in fall and expectant stillness throughout the winter, herbaceous plants embody the spirit of the seasons. Excluding these expressive individuals makes a landscape unnatural; their absence isolates the garden from the rhythm of the seasons. Including them in great sweeps transforms a landscape into what is truly a garden for all seasons; a source of visual delight all year round. The new American garden celebrates the seasons with designs that harness the very forces of nature. Seasonal variations are allowed for, designed for. The rush of spring growth is welcomed, the lushness of summer accommodated, and the spareness of the winter landscape appreciated.

Supporting the new style is a spatial and temporal framework in which exciting combinations of plants express themselves. The result is a garden with a life of its own. Never static, its only constant is change. Tremendous growth, dramatic differences in scale, movement of grasses and wildlife, changes in color and form—all of these elements contribute to dynamic landscaping.

Once established, such a garden begins its own course of evolution, responding to subtle differences in climate, soil, and exposure. Certain plants will dominate, others will hold their own, and still others, unsuitable to the microclimate, may disappear. Grasses, evergreens, and the hardscape—walks, terraces, and pools—hold the garden together, while wild flowers and herbaceous perennials fill out, soften, blossom, camouflage, and surprise. What occurs spontaneously in the surrounding natural landscape takes place by design in these gardens.

Handsome, sturdy, undemanding perennials gathered from around the world combine with native plants selected over millennia by climatic conditions to provide landscaping that is easy to care for, dynamic, sophisticated, and good looking. Within a carefully constructed framework, exciting combinations of plants grow up to express themselves in a new American garden.

Combining the designer's concern for the art of landscaping—the proper placement of landscape elements—with the age-old gardener's delight in the seasonal dynamics of plants, the new American garden carefully includes and precisely places those plants whose self-limiting growth, adaptability, and year-round appearance require minimal upkeep. The new American garden combines practical, no-nonsense American design with sophisticated, beautiful, and very sturdy plantings. Then it allows Nature to take over, to express herself within the unique combination of factors present in an individual garden.

Toward a New American Garden

SINCE STYLE IS always the product of a time and place and history, it should come as no surprise that the American garden arose in the wake of a tremendous wave of gardening interest in the United States. The years between 1970 and 1985 saw a constantly growing and increasingly sophisticated interest in gardening. Garden products proliferated, horticultural publications broadened their scope, catering to an increasingly knowledgeable readership, and at the same time a treasure trove of English gardening expertise became available to the American public.

American gardening enthusiasts devoured information and were as awed by the wealth of the English gardening tradition as they were dismayed that for most Americans climate and life-style made the transplanting of the glorious English perennial and mixed borders impossible. Throughout history the gardens of England and its eighteenth-century colonies have been the role models held up to American gardeners. Only a closer acquaintance with English gardens and more experience in their own backyards have shown gardeners that English gardens must be recognized for what they are: beautiful expressions of another culture, another climate, and another era. Not only don't American geography and climates support these models but they are too cumbersome and labor-intensive for the American life-style.

Colonial Americans followed European styles of gardening because

In a great wave of gardening interest in the United States, Americans experimented with every conceivable new method of gardening. Among these, edible landscaping challenged the existing notion of landscaping as purely ornamental. A blushing pear in a Pennsylvania garden picks up the hues of ornamental plants, demonstrating that beauty and practicality are not mutually exclusive.

they considered themselves Europeans. Their concepts of beauty and, indeed, of civilization were rooted in the Old World. Thus, for a long time Americans could not appreciate their own country's unique beauty. The yardstick with which they measured beauty had been fashioned in a different world. From the point of view of European immigrants coming to the American continent, there was nothing here: "There was nothing but land, not a country at all, but the material out of which countries are made"(*My Ántonia* by Willa Cather).

Native Americans had lived lightly on the land, in peaceful coexistence with nature. In their world view, man was part of a natural community that also included plants and animals. In contrast, European immigrants, laying out gardens at both ends of a vast continent, held entirely different attitudes toward nature and the land. European thought held that man was separate from and above nature. At best he sought to control it; at worst he found it hostile. Land was something to own and use.

The gardens of the Old World told of nature controlled. In seventeenth-century England great houses boasted knot gardens—plants grown in neatly clipped complicated designs—and mazes of evergreen hedges. In France gardens were geometric parterres, reflecting the triumph of Renaissance mathematical thinking. In Spain another kind of geometry prevailed: architectural gardens of Moorish ancestry with long reflecting pools, fountains to cool the air, and elegantly understated walls to cast shadow and provide privacy.

Then, at about the time that European civilization was firmly enough entrenched on the American continent for gardens to be regarded as ornamental in addition to practical, a revolution in gardening taste erupted in England and swept through Europe. Owners of grand old estates ordered the mathematically exacting designs modelled after Versailles plowed under in favor of a natural style embodied in the designs of the foremost English garden designers of their day, Lancelot "Capability" Brown and Humphrey Repton. In keeping with a century that glorified natural science, these gardens were "picturesque landscapes" with copses and sweeping lawn, often embellished with classical ruins or statuary to evoke an emotional response in the beholder. In Colonial America, where the affluent followed the fashions of Europe and especially England, it was this style—the English landscaped park—that was imported. Its permutations, in lawns and evergreen shrubbery, have held sway up to the present.

In Europe the picturesque English landscapes were, in part, expressions of a nostalgia for a pastoral past. In the colonies, by contrast, a sweeping lawn represented a hard-won luxury. It was a sign of progress, a successful transformation from untamed wilderness, an island of order in a sea of magnificent and virile vegetation. In America there was no need to construct a picturesque, awe-inspiring view; it was naturally awe-inspiring. Furthermore, the English landscape, with its picturesque pastoral scenes of long-settled land and gentle vegetation, was impossible to achieve in America. The rugged, virgin country wouldn't be squeezed into the picture.

Today, after two centuries of relentless development, American landscapes often still wear a young, almost wild look. Lush southern vegetation along cypress swamps, arid southwestern vistas in the earthen tones of the long, rainless summer, vast plains covered in rhythmic rows of corn and wheat—all of these landscapes, however different from one another, are distinctively American. Even in rock-studded old New England, giants of forest trees, dwarfing quaint old villages, explode into color in the fall. Nature is too ebullient to fade quietly into winter.

Americans appreciate these vestiges of wilderness more than ever now that they are becoming scarce. They are remnants of the wild, young landscape that once covered the country. In earlier days, however, people held ambivalent attitudes toward the land. On the one hand, they enjoyed the freedom and challenge of its immensity. On the other, the challenge sometimes seemed too great, the freedom, a sign of a complete lack of civilization. In her novel, *O Pioneers*, Willa Cather writes of settlers who homesteaded the Midwest: "But the great fact was the land itself, which seemed to overwhelm the little beginnings of human society that struggled in its sombre waste. . . . Of all the bewildering things about a new country, the absence of human landmarks is one of the most depressing and disheartening." The land was so big and efforts of pioneers so puny in contrast that the bigness, the openness was the adversary, and any efforts to control it, to place it under cultivation, or to build on it were hailed as progress.

In the nineteenth-century dark woods of giant trees and untamed acres were the rule. To many they signified a lack of refinement and a boorishness. Writing in 1850, Andrew Jackson Downing, arbiter of American architectural and gardening taste, prefaced his book, *The Architecture of Country Houses*, with the following:

> With the perception of proportion, symmetry, order and beauty . . .
> comes that refinement of manners which distinguishes a civilized from a
> coarse and brutal people. So long as men are forced to dwell in log huts
> and follow a hunter's life, we must not be surprised at lynch law and the
> use of the bowie knife. But, when smiling lawns and tasteful cottages be-
> gin to embellish a country, we know that order and culture are established.

Downing's writings, including his *Treatise on the Theory and Practise of Landscape Gardening Adapted to North America*, published in 1841, exerted tremendous influence on his countrymen. Eagerly seized by what was a growing and prosperous middle class, his books were cultural how-tos, leading the way to refinement. He envisioned the American home as sacrosanct, a place that "preserves the purity of the nation and invigorates its intellectual powers." To embellish such a home in "correct taste," he advocated of both beautiful and picturesque versions of the English-style landscape with the planting of exotic shrubs and spacious lawn.

The rich, who could employ gardeners, maintained large estates with gardens modelled after European prototypes. But until about 1870, only the rich could afford lawn because it required labor-intensive cutting. Thereafter, the invention of a relatively inexpensive lawn mower ensured that lawn—the more the better—would be a fixture in American gardens. "Smiling lawn," unbroken by fences, stretched from corner to corner of American neighborhoods, from neighborhood to neighborhood, across whole communities. A well-kept lawn and neatly clipped shrubs became necessary accoutrements of middle-class respectability.

At the turn of the century and in the early years of the twentieth century, wealthy Americans took grand tours of Europe, where they educated themselves and saw what no amount of money could buy or build in America: the Old World's artistic past. Returning, the travelers brought back ideas and artifacts to embellish their homes and gardens and link them in spirit to the grand traditions abroad. Dumbarton Oaks, the estate of Mildred and Robert Woods Bliss in Washington, D.C., now administered by Harvard University, is a good example of a house and garden inspired by the grand tour. Designed by Beatrix Jones Ferrand, the gardens closest to the house are a collection of vignettes of the European grand tour, embellished with antique fountains, old French urns, and garden seats.

Other garden "rooms" or "spaces" at Dumbarton Oaks are re-created scenes of beautiful European and mythological legend and places. Melisande's Allée, named for a medieval romance, wanders through spring meadows before it reaches Lover's Lane Pool, itself suggesting a secret villa garden in Caprarola, Italy. Importing European artifacts and re-creating scenes were a way of making tactile the culture that had been captured and brought back to the New World.

Not everybody agreed with the idea that culture had to come from across the Atlantic. In opposition to the Eastern cultural establishment, with its European standards of measurement, voices in the Midwest were raised. "To import to our cities plans from monarchical countries, with their pompous displays, is a fad reflecting on American intellect," wrote Jens Jensen in his philosophical work, *The Clearing*. A Danish-born, self-made landscape designer, Jensen was associated with the Prairie school, a group that sought inspiration from the American land—specifically the great midwestern plains. Architects Louis Sullivan and Frank Lloyd Wright and poet Vachel Lindsay, friends of Jensen, were also associated with this movement.

Jensen was a knowledgeable plantsman who, like that other man from Illinois, Wilhelm Miller, championed the use of native trees, shrubs, and grasses. Like others associated with the Prairie school, Jensen found inspiration in the vast plains, finding in their seemingly endless hori-

Before 1870 and the invention of a relatively inexpensive lawn mower, only the wealthy could afford lawn which required labor-intensive cutting. Thereafter, lawn became the hallmark of middle-class respectability. An 1889 seed catalog cover shows a small child operating the family mower.
(Photo courtesy of Dumbarton Oaks)

zontality a symbol of artistic freedom. His landscape designs feature plants native to the Midwest joined in large communities along watercourses, naturally installed in what Jensen called "prairie rivers." A man ahead of his time, Jensen sought to preserve the natural landscape in an age of rapid growth and development.

The teachings of the Prairie school had a far more lasting influence on the field of architecture than on landscape architecture. By the 1950s, low-slung ranch houses enjoyed enormous popularity, but their landscaping differed little from the traditional style. The natural prairie style probably looked too much like undeveloped land. In *Jens Jensen, the Prairie Spirit*, Alfred Caldwell wrote, "The man who enjoys Kandinski will often have a difficult time with Jensen. He is likely to look at a Jensen landscape and see nothing but a batch of trees." In the common mind, beauty was still being measured with a European yardstick. In the natural landscape beauty was found lacking: ". . . nothing but land . . . the material out of which countries are made."

People needed a clearly recognizable style. Just as earlier generations had turned to Andrew Jackson Downing, home owners of the early twentieth century bought books like *The Natural Style in Landscape Gardening* by Frank Waugh, head of the division of horticulture and a professor of agriculture at Massachusetts Agricultural College in Amherst. He pronounced the use of native plants in landscaping "a fad" whose proponents were predominantly "the tender sex." Waugh also wrote the introduction to *Foundation Planting* by his associate, Leonard H. Johnson. By 1927, when *Foundation Planting* was published, America was a nation of nations. Large cities encompassed dozens of ethnic neighborhoods in which immigrants from a particular country lived, worked, and dreamed. One way to determine the ethnic makeup of any neighborhood in an American city, it was said, was to look at its garden and window boxes. If they were full of flowers and vegetables, the occupants might well be recent arrivals from Europe or blacks from the rural South. Because the middle class had been steeped in Downing's versions of landscape of "correct taste" or perhaps because they wished to emphasize their status, Americans of longer standing took care to cultivate what they deemed "American" landscaping.

Pressure to assimilate and do things the American way was exerted on immigrants and the children of immigrants. In the introduction to *Foundation Planting*, the "right" sort of landscaping is deemed patriotic.

It is only fair to say that the home is the greatest institution in America. . . . Everyone who is patriotic, therefore, and wants to do something for his country will promote to the utmost of his ability the development of . . . ideal American homes. . . . In the Old Country the primary planting . . . is a hedge all along the street front. The American home . . . is open to the street. The plantings, instead of forming a hedge on the street line, are pushed back against the foundations of the house. They are foundation plantings. This type of planting is therefore fundamental to the whole of

American domestic landscape architecture. . . . It is well and sadly known
. . . that tens of thousands of individual homes have not been planted.
. . . We may all accept the . . . patriotic duty . . . of promoting this cam-
paign of planting.

The American way called for uniformity of landscape design: no fences
or hedges, only foundation plantings and lawn. Anything else was
vaguely unpatriotic and morally suspect. "It is hardly desirable in most
situations to have beds of flowering perennials in front of the house or
included as a part of the foundation planting," Waugh wrote. Even tulips were relegated to the "garden side of the house." Instead of a richness of diversity of garden styles in vastly different geographical areas,
there was a tyranny of conformity. All followed the fashion of the eastern United States, with its long tradition of English influence. Giving
no thought to climatic change, settlers moving west brought with them
notions of gardening that were developed originally in England and
succeeded marginally in the East but were totally unsuitable to the
Southwest and most of the West.

"The settlers knew what America should look like, so they proceeded
to transform California into it using a skewed image of their home landscape back east, ignoring the strange, yet well adapted examples left by
the Spanish and Mexican predecessors," wrote Deborah Ryan in *The
Garden in the Desert*. To sustain eastern plants in the West and Southwest, water was used lavishly. It seemed as inexhaustible as the cheap
gasoline used to power the lawn mowers. Newly developed chemical
fertilizers and pesticides were hailed as miracle products to change the
face of agriculture and horticulture.

After a brief period of restraint during World War II, when concrete
was sometimes dramatically torn up for victory gardens, development
increased on an exponential curve. The great exodus to the suburbs
began. Later, television reinforced the ideal of a single-family home in
the suburbs with a big lawn. No matter what the annual rainfall or
native flora, landscaping differed little if at all from the patriotic landscaping Waugh proselytized: foundation planting along the front of the
house and, of course, lawn.

The 1950s brought two new additions to the typical American property. A new trend for outdoor living resulted in the installation of
thronelike barbecues as adjuncts to terraces, and driveways leading to
garages or carports took up some of the space previously devoted to
lawn. To reach suburban communities whose growth had outstripped
that of public transportation, the car had become a necessity. To accommodate the cars, highways, freeways, beltways, and expressways were
built. By the mid fifties, the "two-car family" was no longer a status
symbol but a reality, and commuting had become a way of life.

One of the first landscape architects to design residential properties
that addressed this new life-style was Californian Thomas Church. His

Mixing together the practical and beautiful, landscape architect Thomas Church designed this California garden for active outdoor living. He believed and wrote that gardens are for people to live in and to use, not simply to admire. Functional elements such as paving and a swimming pool add to the beauty of this landscape.

residential plans integrated spaces for eating outdoors, swimming, parking cars, and storing tools—all on small residential lots. He recognized that for most people a formal garden and gardener were outmoded luxuries, and he created terraces, patios, decks, and planting space that home owners could maintain themselves. Work space, tool storage, and clothes-drying yards for the do-it-yourselfers were frequently included in his plans. He believed and wrote that "gardens are for people." The lot on which the house sat was put to use as an extended living and storage area.

In the booming growth years after World War II, more landscape architects applied their training in the allocation of space to residential properties. Working on a small scale made it necessary to focus on small details, however, and a landscape architect's knowledge of plants—or lack of it—became quickly obvious. In the United States the field of landscape architecture has traditionally concerned itself with the modulation of space rather than horticulture. A student of landscape architecture trained in the fifties might commit to memory a list of suitable "plant material" and spend the rest of his life working with a hundred or so trees and evergreen woody ornamentals suitable to local conditions. This resulted in good use of space but repetitious plantings. Although ground covers of uniform, low plants later became popular for their ability to lessen upkeep and cover sloping and other difficult areas, the basic formula for American landscaping remained the same: foundation planting, a tree or two, and lawn. The idea of lawn was too deeply entrenched in the American psyche to be eliminated. Thus, most designs were for well-apportioned living space outdoors with neat and somewhat monotonous evergreen plantings.

The backyard as extended living area, however, appealed to the practical streak in Americans, who adapted happily to life out of doors. As the yard became an outdoor room, the need for creating privacy through the use of hedges and fences arose, dealing a blow to the old taboo against fencing. Patios, terraces, and decks became popular for the comfort they afforded underfoot. Lawn furniture was added to the growing list of backyard paraphernalia, to be packed into the shed or garage for winter storage—alongside the clippers, lawn mower, barbecue, and DDT.

After the publication of *Silent Spring* by Rachel Carson in 1962, concern for pollution in the environment rose. People began to question the practice of routinely spraying with chemicals for all garden problems. Commonly used pesticides were found to endanger wildlife: Exposure to DDT was found to inhibit the mechanism of some birds to produce the eggshell crucial to propagation of the species, and among the birds so affected was the American eagle. A growing number of wildlife, lakes, and rivers fell victim to pollution, and an energy crunch in the early seventies forced people to reconsider practices that were both wasteful and damaging to the environment.

The American bubble of endless resources and a quick—often chemical—solution to every garden problem had burst. Indiscriminate use of pesticides, the idea of a convenient spray for every bug, was seen to be not only potentially destructive to the environment but fallacious and possibly pathogenic. Gardeners realized that the price of supporting plants and lawn that needed shoring up in alien environments with chemicals and constant irrigation, trimming, and clipping was extortionary.

Interest in and experimentation with organic methods of gardening were part of a great wave of garden interest that began around 1970, in reaction to an increasingly synthetic, chemical world. By 1985, when the National Gardening Association hired the Gallup Organization to poll the nation, it found that "gardening ranks as America's Number 1 outdoor leisure activity. More households garden than jog, play golf, or sail combined."

Tremendous interest in gardening fueled and was refueled by increasingly sophisticated offerings. Garden products of every description, including those that worked with Nature instead of against her, were available. Natural predators like the praying mantis and the ladybug could be ordered by telephone and paid for by credit card. A renewed interest in native plants ultimately raised the national consciousness to an awareness and an appreciation of the wealth and beauty of its own flora. From Germany, a highly industrialized nation that greatly values its natural-style gardens, came new hybrids of ornamental grasses, outstanding perennial hybrids, and the concept of demonstration gardens—public gardens where new plants and plant combinations were displayed for home gardeners to see and try.

American garden publications abounded. Some, like *The Complete Book of Edible Landscaping* by Rosalind Creasy, challenged the notion of residential landscaping as solely ornamental. In addition to American books on virtually every gardening subject from no-work gardens to gardens of fragrance, the best English garden books—including new editions of classics by such giants of English gardening as Gertrude Jeckyll, William Robinson, and Vita Sackville-West— became available in America. Ironically, familiarity with the source books of modern British gardening as well as a hands-on understanding of garden dynamics has turned Americans away from traditional mentors in search of a new truly American-style garden.

Arboreta that once displayed only English-style herbaceous borders and traditional garden plants are devoting space to native plants. At the Morton Arboretum in Illinois and the Shaw Arboretum in Missouri, stands of native prairie grow. At River Farm, the home of the American Horticultural Society in Virginia, and at the National Arboretum in Washington, D.C., there are meadow plantings. The Denver Botanic Garden recently installed what it can grow better than any arboretum in the country: a rock alpine garden designed by Herb Schaal of Edaw, Inc., a landscape architectural firm that specializes in low-water-use and climate-appropriate gardens.

Instead of looking abroad, landscape designers around the country are looking around them and finding inspiration in the American landscape. Connecticut landscape architect A. E. Bye's exquisite perception of the American landscape is expressed in designs so perfectly in harmony with their surroundings that they are impossible to distinguish from nature. The extravagant use of herbaceous material by the Washington- and Baltimore-based firm of Oehme, van Sweden & Associates ties designs to the rhythmic cycle of the seasons. Arizona landscape architect Steve Martino's low-water-use designs respect the desert's singular beauty. Research and restoration of Wisconsin prairies conducted by Darrel Morrison provide startlingly beautiful, low-maintenance landscaping for structures on the Wisconsin prairie. These refreshing new gardens are milestones along the way to a new American garden.

Educated in the gardening revolution, designers as well as sophisticated, knowledgeable home owners are adjusting eyes and minds to a new garden that arises from the natural surroundings. As the natural landscape that surrounds our housing disappears, the longing for untrammeled nature increases. There is a great American nostalgia for the land as it once was. In addition to all the other qualities Americans demand of their gardens—sophistication, easily maintained good looks, an outside living area surrounded with lush vegetation—the new garden has to provide what is missing from daily experience. The new garden must restore to contemporary lives the spontaneity and beauty of the American countryside.

An American inferiority complex that manifested itself in sterile, rigidly conformist lawn and foundation planting landscaping and copies of European gardens is disappearing as knowledgeable, sophisticated gardeners learn to appreciate what is unique in the American landscape. In this Connecticut garden, landscape architect A. E. Bye restored the beauty of a natural bog.
(Photo courtesy of A. E. Bye)

Dynamic Combinations in Time and Space

I N H A R M O N Y with the natural world, the new American garden is dynamic, a space in a constant state of change. No longer a static evergreen set piece, the new garden is a place of movement, deriving dynamism from the life cycles of herbaceous plants included in great number. These plants and their changing relationships to trees, bulbs, and evergreens convey the message of the seasons: emergence in spring, fullness in summer, and a gradual golden thinning out in fall. In winter there is an expectant stillness until, one by one, the plants come back from the dead—a springtime event as reliable as it is amazing. In their resurrection and prodigious growth, herbaceous plants provide movement and drama in the garden.

Each herbaceous plant's predictable schedule of emergence, growth, bloom, and demise plays out over the seasons in a kind of visual melody. When combined with other perennials, bulbs, evergreens, and ornamental grasses of complementary but different schedules of development, the result is a New World symphony for the eyes—nostalgic and evocative of the American past, of wilderness and prairie, of wheat fields and rural pleasures.

Old-style green gardens, composed only of evergreens and lawn, stayed the same regardless of season, looking artificial and removed from the natural world. Today, landscaping need no longer be static. Home owners and gardeners across the country are loosening their death grip on

Viewed from the ground in early May, the stylized meadow features mid-season and late tulips that extend the period of bloom after daffodils *(background)* have finished. Emerging ornamental grass, calamagrostis, and the new growth of epimedium camouflage bulbs' foliage.

painstakingly maintained lawn and evergreens that stay the same day after day, season after season; instead, they are taking pleasure in the ephemeral nature of the garden.

A new attitude—at once easier and more comfortable with natural processes than ever before—supports the new style. The gardener intervenes in the natural course of events by installing a community of plants suited to his site. After that, nature is manipulated as little as

Landscaping with bulbs, perennials, and ornamental grasses ties a garden to the rhythmic progression of the seasons. All of the photos in this chapter show seasonal changes in the same highly stylized meadow at the Virginia Avenue Garden in Washington, D.C., designed by Oehme, van Sweden & Associates. Some photos were taken from the top floor of the Federal Reserve Bank Building looking down, while others show the same planting at ground level.

April: Spring brings a burst of bloom from bergenias, daffodils, hyacinths, and early tulips. Large rings are ornamental grasses, *Miscanthus sinensis* and *M. sinensis* 'Gracillimus,' which will rise to prominence after the bulbs fade.

May: Bright new growth of epimediums all but engulfs spent daffodil foliage. Deeper green liriope surrounds late tulips. Ornamental grasses have begun their rapid growth.

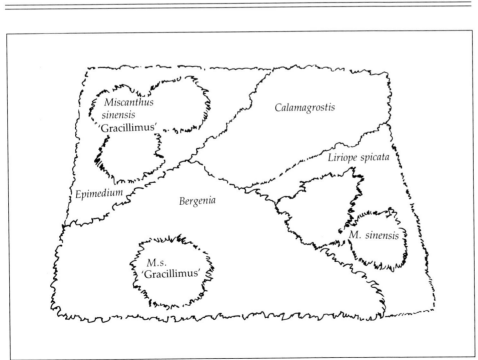

June: Bulbs are finished, and ground covers, epimediums, liriope, and grasses have grown lush and full, masking their dying foliage.

possible. Because plants are allowed to grow into natural forms, labor-intensive control by clipping, trimming, and cutting is unnecessary. With fresh, tolerant eyes the gardener not only accepts but designs for all of the stages of a plant's cycle. Flowers are not always in bloom. Seed heads form. Plants wither to coppery brown and taupe. Frost kills. Winter brings new dimensions. All of these phenomena are accepted in the new garden. Tolerant eyes do not expect to see impeccably manicured

September: Hot late-summer sunshine turns epimediums bronze and begins to blush bergenias to rose.

October: Fall brings slowly changing colors. The field of bergenias blushes rose while that of epimediums turns coppery brown. Grasses begin to bloom.

lawn and ceaseless greenery. They find beauty—in seed heads, frost-struck grasses, the distinctive lines of a leafless tree—carefully planned for fall and winter appeal.

Far from an antiseptic landscape that isolates itself from seasonal variation, the new garden celebrates the seasons, finding special beauty in each month of the year. The word "garden" takes on a larger meaning, referring not only to extravagant shows of summer blooming perennials but to the slow turning of leaves in the fall and to the wisps of grass heads poking through the snow. It refers to the changing relationship of plant to plant within the garden.

Evergreens no longer dominate the landscape but relate to dynamic herbaceous plants in different ways throughout the year. In summer, when they are an all-but-invisible backdrop behind layers of other plants, evergreens add dark-green depth to the garden. In autumn they gain increasing prominence as colors around them fade and flame. In winter evergreens come into their own as their deep lustrous color combines stunningly with the frost-touched almonds and wheats of ornamental grasses.

In the new garden the same relationship of plant to plant, of deciduous to herbaceous to evergreen, that occurs in nature is highly concentrated for viewing pleasure. Plants that augment and epitomize each season's special beauty are carefully placed and used in quantity. For many city dwellers the day in, day out view from the kitchen or living room window is the sole experience with the world of nature. When that view is of dynamic ground cover that rearranges itself into a seasonal tableaux, it nourishes the soul.

A changing show outside the window is assured ahead of time by selecting precisely those dynamic herbaceous and other plants whose habits are suitable for these gardens. Those that die gracefully, with attractive seed heads or glorious winter color, those whose period of bloom is long and lovely, those whose attractive foliage works in beautiful combinations for attractive ground cover, and those with an especially early or dramatic spring bloom are excellent candidates.

In many parts of the country early-blooming small trees start off the gardening year. Witch hazel *(Hamamelis mollis)* blooms in fragrant yellow corkscrews in late winter. Spike winter hazel *(Corylopsis spicata),* another late winter bloomer, boasts yellow bell-shaped flowers even before the earliest bulbs.

A burst of blooming bulbs announces spring with color and excitement. Bulbs belong in the new garden. They give much and demand little. The earliest—snowdrops, winter aconites, and snow crocuses—are the smallest, creating spectacular results when used in vast quantity. Crocuses or snowdrops by the hundreds or even thousands instead of merely dozens present an early season display that will linger in the memory. They don't have to be planted all at once. It is easier on both back and pocketbook to plant a few dozen each year. The dif-

At eye level in the summer garden, ornamental grasses, *Miscanthus sinensis* 'Gracillimus' and calamagrostis, punctuate interlocking fields of ground cover. At left foreground is *Bergenia cordifolia* and at right, *Liriope spicata*.

ficult part will be remembering the overall picture and sticking to a single type and color in the face of tempting displays at the garden center. It is always better to plant multiples of a single type than to plant small numbers of mixed colors and types. Smatterings of purples, whites, blues, and yellows are cheerful and colorful but cancel one another out. A quarter-acre given over entirely to yellow crocus or bright blue chiondoxa, however, is a sight that will continue to bloom for the inward eye.

Daffodils, Atamasco lilies, hyacinths, and summer-blooming bulbs like giant allium all have a place in the garden. Once planted, bulbs perform for years. Their blooming time becomes an event to be anticipated. An exception to the rule of permanence are tulips, which provide exciting marvelous color in May but are a bit more difficult than other bulbs and require yearly replanting for best effect. Sometimes they persist for decades; at other times they won't bloom a second year. Because of their impermanence, they are good subjects for the gardener to use in color experiments. Their blooming time and wonderful display are worth the effort in planting them.

After blooming, all bulbs form unsightly, sprawling foliage that must be left on the plant to ensure the following year's flowers. Unfortunately, the bigger the bulb, the messier its demise. When grown among groups of perennials that emerge and send forth new spring growth even before the flowers fade, however, this after-bloom sprawl is not as noticeable. Selecting plants that perform just as the bulbs fade is the key to keeping the new garden as lively as it is good looking.

Fortunately, the blooming of bulbs dovetails beautifully with the first appearance of many perennials. The delicate apple green of emerging grasses such as calamagrostis, pennisetum, and miscanthus makes a stunning ground cover for brilliant tulips. The deep matte green foliage of *Rudbeckia fulgida* 'Goldsturm' carpets the ground around vibrant hyacinths and tulips. Brilliant epimedium climbs the stalk of still-blooming daffodils. One summer-blooming bulb that persists attractively as a dried flower ball is the giant allium. Left on their stalks, alliums punctuate a meadow planting of smaller grasses with silvery beige balls.

Planning the succession of bulbs, herbaceous plants, and grasses demands careful attention. Bulbs make it easy to get a burst of color in spring. Planning for subsequent seasons takes a bit more thought. Restraint in the number of different kinds of plants comes into the picture here. In an old-fashioned perennial border, many plants are used and look fine. The border is surrounded by plain green lawn; it is a small subject of interest in a large, monochromatic matrix. When subjects of the border are used to cover all of the ground, the rules change. Fewer kinds of perennials are used, but they are planted in greater numbers. They join together in horizontal masses whose uniformity is relieved by occasional tall, bold specimens.

Massing perennials at a scale effective in the landscape calls for only a few kinds of plants, but each one must have "the right stuff." It must

At ground level, a blooming miscanthus dominates a field of blushing bergenias. Drying epimediums have begun the slow passage into winter.

be a superior individual—attractive and effective longer than other plants with a more extended, showier period of bloom. It shouldn't clash but should neatly dovetail with and complement the display of other plants. Not every plant falls into this category. In choosing combinations that are effective over a long period, complementary colors and shapes, dovetailing bloom, overall appearance throughout the growing season, winter aspect, and length of blooming time are the deciding factors. In addition to choosing plants that appeal over time, plants in the new garden are chosen to fit perfectly into a given space. By covering the ground and filling the space, they edge out weeds. Those selected are self-limiting: Of predictable height and proportions, they won't outgrow their allotted spaces. Rather than cutting back a plant to suit a

Cold weather brings out different hues. Cold blushes bergenias purple as it blanches the grasses into bright dried-flower bouquets.

space, the gardener selects plants with the built-in qualities he wants so that care after planting is minimized.

Because it is part of an overall design, each stage of a perennial's development must be attractive. Foliage that is good looking when the plant is not in bloom is a necessity. The length and profusion of bloom is another factor to consider. Attractive seed pods and flower bracts that add interest in fall and winter are other desirable attributes.

Achilleas, astilbes, threadleaf coreopsis, ceratostigmas, 'Autumn Joy' sedums, and 'Goldsturm' rudbeckias are all plants with an extremely long period of appeal. By April these plants will have begun to grow fresh new leaves. Each has a long, showy period of bloom and attractive foliage throughout the growing season. Seed heads or bracts of their showy flowers, left on the plants, provide a second, more subdued period of interest in fall and winter. Some plants are grown primarily for their foliage. Among these are hostas and sweet woodruff, both of which disappear in winter. Liriope, which stays green, has lavender blue flowers in midsummer followed by shiny black berries. The distinctive foliage of epimediums and bergenias responds to light and temperature, blushing rose in the summer sun and turning shades of bronze after frost.

Large masses of herbaceous material of uniform height are broken—for interest's sake—with single specimens or small groups of plants that are distinctive enough in their own right to have impact. These plants have presence. Tall plume poppies *(Macleaya cordata)*, Japanese blood grass *(Imperata cylindrica rubra* 'Red Baron'), and virtually all ornamental grasses are among the best of plants with presence.

Ornamental grasses are ideal candidates for the new garden in other ways as well. While their robust, rapid growth to great size and volume lends excitement to the garden, they are well behaved giants that do not overgrow their spaces. Like no other herbaceous plant, large ornamental grasses lend volume to the garden, dramatically altering space. With their rapid growth, the spare beauty of early spring swiftly becomes a summer jungle of lush density. Many grasses bloom in fall when little else is blooming. Their greatest contribution, however, is made in winter, when frost transforms soft greens to shades of apricot, wheat, and almond.

While the giants provide magnificent accents, smaller grasses serve as elegant high ground cover whose great charms are musical, rustling movement and lacy, delicate seed heads. From the first frost to late February when grasses are cut back, they provide glowing winter interest that is as showy and full as that of summer flowers. Contrasting with evergreens, they appear as giant bouquets of dried flowers, riveting the observer's attention throughout the winter.

Larger grasses are outstanding winter specimens. One of the finest large ornamental grasses is Eulalia grass *(Miscanthus sinensis)* and its varieties. Leaves of Eulalia grass are a clean, dusty green that rustle softly with every breeze. The generous proportions of Eulalia grass, which continues to grow in width as it ages, give a wonderful density to summer gardens. In winter its almond-colored foliage contrasts strikingly with that of evergreens. Giant *Miscanthus floridulus* grows to ten feet and more when conditions are right. Blades are flat and ribbonlike. In places with long growing seasons, giant miscanthus bears white plumes in late summer. Clumps of this grass make spectacular screens.

Smaller ornamental grasses combine well with flowers of meadow origin such as rudbeckia and echinacea. Masses of low-growing grasses—such as panicum and pennisetum—are some of the few herbaceous plants that retain dense volume throughout winter. Even when planted on a grid, their loose, easy foliage impresses as spontaneous and natural. Plants in the new garden are unclipped, unmowed, and untrimmed. Not only is the natural form less work, it is more attractive. Blowing, natural forms satisfy the heart's—and eye's—nostalgia for prairie and field.

The photos and charts in this chapter show combinations of magnificent ground cover and how they function over the gardening year. All aspects of a plant's development are considered: the way it looks as it emerges and first begins to grow, how and when it blooms and with what other plants, and how it appears after frost. Far from a comprehensive group of plants, the ones included are only a few of the good plants that have long periods of bloom, are broadly adaptable, and are appealing before bloom and attractive in winter. Along with grasses, these long-lasting, exceptional plants function as structure in a planting—backing up less enduring material. Outstanding perennials combine with bulbs, wild flowers, grasses, and ferns as opulent ground cover that functions in time as well as in space. Using this material in abundance is the single most important element of the new style because it dramatically augments seasonal changes.

No longer packed into tight rectangles of traditional perennial border, herbaceous plants spill out over the landscape in masses that divide themselves along patterns of light, shade, soil type, and moisture conditions. Great sweeps of continually changing colors signal the passage of the seasons.

Thus, the new garden delights throughout the year. There is no off season, and there is always something to see. The view from the window shows a new American garden as ephemeral as music. Each perennial plant emerges in its location on its own schedule. It unfolds, reaches up, fills out, blooms, and withers in harmony with the plants around it. Like the sound made by a single instrument in an orchestra, its development follows the melody but expresses the music in a unique way. What begins in the still, sparse beauty of winter quickens in the earliest spring with the first flowers. As spring progresses, each new emerging group of plants delights with a slow unfolding, a show of blossoms that gives way in its turn to another successively unfolding, blossoming group.

Summer is a buxom season of ripeness bursting to maturity that thins slowly and irrevocably into autumn. When plants no longer grow up and out, the big grasses' constant undulation keeps movement and sound in the garden.

Easy-care, nostalgic, and dynamic, this landscaping must be planned over time as well as in space. Planning the new garden involves working into the design a succession of what is picturesque in each season. The garden is tied to the natural surroundings by using a color palette as broad as the hues of nature: pale new green, vivid gold, scintillating scarlet, melancholy autumn burgundy, winter white.

Control over the plants' sizes and shapes is exerted before planting, not afterwards by maintenance. Informed selection and thoughtful placement of self-limiting plants enable them to grow freely, without constant intervention. Unmowed, unclipped, unstaked, they relate to one another and follow their own patterns of development. The result is a lively, spontaneous, easy-care series of changing tableaux.

Plants that can be left to their own devices create a spontaneous landscape that evokes memories of a uniquely American past. The best metaphor for this new garden is prairie—a hip-high community of contrasting but complementary plants that functions as a beautifully integrated whole. Like a prairie, the new garden changes daily: flowers bloom, grasses go to seed—not by ones and twos but by hundreds, even thousands. Extravagant massing punctuated by trees, giant grasses, and stately perennials mimics nature's magnificent abundance. Combinations that suit their situations without constant intervention to shore up, to control or to restrain allow the plants and the garden to recapture a sense of nature's spontaneity.

Dried grasses are effective all winter. Poking through snow, almond-colored seed heads sparkle in the dying winter sunlight.

Meaningful Maintenance

I would suggest that the trend toward low maintenance has now become a necessity.

—Thomas Church

Don't call it maintenance-free—there's no such thing!

—Wolfgang Oehme

There's a certain amount of housekeeping in any garden.

—Christopher Friedrichs

To the good gardener all kinds of design are good if not against the site, soil, climate, or labours of his garden—a very important point, the last.

—William Robinson

ALL OF THE EXPERTS agree: Gardens of any kind need maintenance. There is no such thing as a work-free garden. The question shouldn't really be "How much work is it?" but, rather, "What do you get for the time you spend?" Does the garden repay its owner for time spent by providing pleasure and a respite from the world? Or is the yard a square of grass bordered by evergreen shrubs—indistinguishable from every other yard, and demanding a mindless routine of busywork that is as challenging and interesting as vacuuming a rug?

One of the biggest reasons for the perpetuation of traditional landscaping, with lawn and a foundation planting of evergreen shrubs, is that it requires practically no knowledge of plants or planting. Since everybody does it and has done it for so long, there is advice in abundance. Companies producing fertilizers publish literature detailing when and what to spread. The rest—mowing and trimming—is busywork, time-consuming but not mentally taxing. The result, however, is a landscape that is neat, artificially green, and aesthetically deadening, a garden that satisfies outmoded convention but slowly starves the soul.

More than ever in today's mechanized urban society, gardens are a precious link to the natural world. In urban landscapes and in lives bereft of natural beauty, gardens bear the heavy burden of supplying all the beauty, melancholy, and mystery of that world. In an era when people have less time and little inclination to spend leisure in time-consuming upkeep, gardens are more looked at and looked into than ever before. Today's garden is also more closely related to the house, more necessary as an extended living area, and more vital to people as a window on the world of nature. Social and economic patterns have changed; for households in which all adult members work outside the home and for home owners who cannot afford to hire outside help for their gardens, the need for low maintenance is as great as the longing for beauty.

Having the beauty of a new American garden and the ease of a low-maintenance landscape requires a little physical and a lot of mental energy. Establishing the new garden takes learning about some unfamiliar plants and their growth requirements, requires a more liberal attitude toward the various stages of a plant's life cycle, and involves preventive maintenance.

In installing a new garden, the first decision a gardener has to make is whether or not to have or keep lawn. This is a difficult one for most Americans, who have a long and unquestioned tradition of lawn and evergreens as landscaping. Lawn has always been an important inclusion in American landscaping. Early in our history it symbolized the triumph of civilization over wilderness. Later it was evocative of refinement and beauty. But today the inclusion of lawn in landscaping has become merely reflexive. Whether lawn is useful is seldom considered; we simply find it hard to break the lawn habit. Instead of just assuming that lawn will be included in a landscape, people must learn to ask "What will I do with it—besides mow and trim it?" "Will it be necessary for croquet, football?" and "Is the occasional game worth the time and expense involved in maintaining turf?"

Lawn as ground cover needs labor-intensive work—at the least, weekly cutting throughout the growing season. In many areas it also requires irrigation. Its maintenance needs make it a low priority in the new garden.

Those who cannot quite bring themselves to eliminate lawn would do well to limit it to an easily handled oval surrounded by perennial ground cover. In this way areas that need trimming after the grass is cut—on slopes, around trees and shrubs, and next to paths—will be blanketed with magnificent, labor-saving ground cover.

Illustration labels: *Magnolia virginiana*, *Ivy*, *Mahonia*, *Miscanthus floridulus*, *Calamagrosti x acutiflora stricta*, *Brunnera*, *Liriope spicata*, *Bergenia*

Eliminating lawn, if only in the backyard, will yield much more room for living and garden areas. The space can be divided into only two parts: hardscape (paving, paths, and parking) and a new landscape (magnificent ground cover). Both can be expansive. Both make maintaining the garden easy and enjoying it a certainty.

Paving provides both a ground cover requiring extremely little maintenance and a garden element that is good looking in all seasons. It can be a patio, a path, or even a pool. It directs circulation, defines use areas, and furnishes a firm surface for outdoor activity. It can be a garden feature that contrasts with the softness of plantings. Paved surfaces provide ample room for walking, sitting, and eating; thus, the planted areas of the garden are protected from traffic. Stone and brick paving are virtually indestructible and require only occasional sweeping as maintenance. Decking requires an annual treatment to keep wood in good condition. Handsome, weather-resistant surfaces extend what is man-made into the natural, serving as transition from inside to out.

The "hardscape," the paved area, should be commodious enough to accommodate whatever gathering will occur: neighborhood or office

Measuring only seventeen by fifty-five feet, designer James van Sweden's tiny city garden requires minimal upkeep in exchange for a lush and constantly changing view of the natural world. Ground covers, paving, and handsome, sturdy plants with the right stuff require little maintenance. The white spiggot indicates that an underground irrigation system has been installed. In the foreground, *Liriope spicata*, *Bergenia cordifolia*, and *Brunnera macrophylla* mingle around the sculptural trunks of a *Magnolia virginiana*. Placing a large specimen, kept open by high pruning, in the foreground enhances the sense of depth. Giant alliums provide color.

Pools are a most beautiful and exotic way of covering the ground. A bridge of decking leads across a pool that covers virtually all of the ground in this small urban garden. Pools are also maintenance bargains, adding a new dimension to a garden, attracting wildlife, supporting different kinds of plant life, and adding attractive ground cover that requires very little upkeep. A shed serves as a screen to block the view of neighboring houses as well as provide a place to store plants and tools for the owner's hobby, bonsai.
(Design by Christopher Friedrichs)

Dividing the space into two—paving and areas of plants with the right stuff—keeps upkeep to a minimum while making the garden a place of delight. In the foreground of this Maryland garden, *Bergenia cordifolia, Rudbeckia fulgida* 'Goldsturm,' and pachysandra cover the ground. In the background, behind a border of *Ceratostigma plumbaginoides* and silvery *Stachys byzantina*, a mass of *Sedum telephium* 'Autumn Joy' blooms in October.

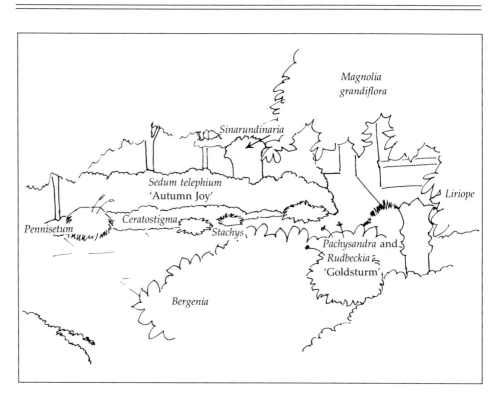

parties, family reunions, outdoor dinner parties, outdoor living. A space that is the size of a small indoor room will look cramped outside. Bigger spaces relate to the sky, tall trees, and the exterior of the house.

Choose the largest possible paved area that still leaves room for planting. Install paving in places convenient to exterior doors. Outdoor living spaces that are removed from the house by long stairways or woodland paths make good trysting spots but are otherwise generally underused.

Garden pools are a different way of covering the ground with paving. They are maintenance bargains, offering great beauty and pleasure in return for minimal upkeep. Pools supply a view when there is none in sight. They attract wildlife and support a whole new realm of plants and water creatures.

Once the paved areas are in place, it is time to plant. But even a new American garden has to fall back on the age-old precept: soil preparation first. Taking care that the soil is in good tilth—which may require the addition of peat moss, humus, sand, or compost—is the ounce of preparation worth the pound of cure. Plants grown in good soil are larger, healthier, more resistant to disease, and longer-lived than those grown in poor media.

Because the new garden relies on perennial plants—those that winter over and live for years—the importance of an all-out, thoroughgoing preparation of the soil before planting cannot be overemphasized. This is not an easy job, of course, but rather an enormous amount of work. Doing a good job before planting, however, will allow for years of easier maintenance afterwards. Plants will be robust, healthy, and able to crowd out weeds and withstand the vicissitudes of weather.

A layer of mulch is a ground covering that will slowly decompose and add humus to the soil as it conserves moisture and keeps down weeds. Fallen leaves add nutrients and function as a mulch; they may be left in place if their appearance is not objectionable and they do not smother evergreen material.

In the last two decades ground covers, such as pachysandra, ajuga, and creeping junipers, have been touted as the cure-all to maintenance problems. Ground covers certainly crowd out weeds and keep the ground shaded and thus more moist, but most of the common ones remain the same all year round. Neat beds of pachysandra and ivy are easy but not exciting. Generally, they grow so low to the ground that they are effective only along the ground plane—in two dimensions. Ground cover doesn't have to be low. Tall ground cover is effective not only on the ground plane but in the third dimension. Nor need ground cover be evergreen. When composed of large numbers of a single herbaceous perennial or an interesting combination of herbaceous perennials, ground cover stops being merely static green. In the natural landscape, meadows and prairies are spontaneously occurring masses of herbaceous plants. The color, height, and volume of these masses are constantly changing, creating tension and excitement in the landscape. When the same masses are planted in the garden, the result is dynamic landscaping.

Sophisticated gardeners want more from their yards than ever. As land becomes more precious, gardens are smaller and what little remains becomes all the more valuable as living and inspirational space. In what is often a soulless wilderness of shopping centers, parking lots, and heavily trafficked streets, city and suburban dwellers look to their gardens not only as additional living space but as a window on the natural world. Covering the ground with great sweeps of exciting, ever-changing herbaceous plants makes such a garden a natural retreat, a place of excitement in which there is always something happening.

Because the new garden counts on the performance of herbaceous plants, it is of utmost importance to buy exactly those plants that are high performers, the kind the great German horticulturist Karl Foerster called *Ornungshelden*, "class heroes." These are plants a cut above the rest: trouble-free, outstanding individuals that always look good, that succeed without mollycoddling. These are plants with the "right stuff." Learning and using their Latin names will avoid disappointing sound-alikes. Many plants, for example, go by the name of black-eyed Susan, among them gangly annual flowers that bloom fleetingly and go swiftly to seed. But there is only one *Rudbeckia fulgida* 'Goldsturm,' a good-looking, true perennial that blooms for two months on stocky, deep green plants. After bloom, masses of chocolate-colored seed heads provide another, more subdued period of show.

Another outstanding example is *Sedum telephium* 'Autumn Joy.' It appears in April as a tidy mound of succulent foliage that stays neat and compact throughout the growing season. In summer, showy umbels of lettuce-green buds open to dusty pink flowers that finally darken to copper-colored seed, a process that takes a full three months. Unless overfed, 'Autumn Joy' remains compact and does not require staking. It is healthy, unbothered by fungus or insects, and when seed heads are left on the plants, attractive far into winter. The seed heads are particularly attractive poking through the snow. Using masses of a plant like 'Autumn Joy' means eleven months of garden interest with little, if any, work.

Ornamental grasses are, by nature, plants with the right stuff. They are attractive from the moment they emerge from the ground and camouflage the dying foliage of bulbs. They require no busywork—no staking, clipping, or pruning—and they never outgrow their spaces. Most of them flower and hold their seed heads heads far into fall when little else is blooming. In winter, frost transforms ornamental grasses into giant dried flower bouquets.

Using only those plants that are head and shoulders above the others is a way of maintaining the garden ahead of time. Potential maintenance work is planned out of the garden, before plants are even placed in the ground.

Finding the more dynamic kinds of ground cover used in the new American garden can be challenging. First of all, most nurseries will not group rudbeckias, astilbes, or achilleas with more common ground covers; when available locally, most will be found among the perennials. And ornamental grasses, while gaining in popularity, may still be hard to find. Furthermore, the new garden uses plants commonly considered to be border subjects in masses and numbers generally associated with standard kinds of ground cover like ivy. The appendix lists mail order sources for plants suggested in this book.

Besides soil and plants, water is necessary for healthy gardens. After the soil has been improved and before the plants are put into place, take time to consider whether the installation of an irrigation system is worth the money and effort. Though plants in the new garden are carefully selected for their suitability and stamina, even the toughest varieties need watering during times of drought. Whether they will be watered by an irrigation system or a garden hose at those times is a matter of convenience and price.

In regions of the country with dry seasons, irrigation is necessary for virtually any type of plant but cacti and succulents. In recent years the concept of "xeriscape," or low-water-use landscape, has generated interest. Xeriscape designs call for plants and grasses that can grow in semi-arid climates found in the American Southwest without much—if any—supplementary water. Gardeners in areas that suffer periodic water shortages or where future water shortages threaten should investigate what promises to be an intriguing and very beautiful approach to landscaping.

Each individual garden is composed of several microclimates or cultural niches that are determined by a complex series of characteristics, ranging from latitude and longitude to relationship to house walls and fences. Plant health and performance rely on a correct fit of plant to the appropriate microclimate. The new garden uses plants that suit its cultural niches and whose appearance is in keeping with the surrounding vegetation. For example, wooded sites call for woodland plants, very often those occurring naturally on the site. But ornamental perennials that are not native to American woodlands such as ligularia and hostas are suitable to wooded sites because they come from similar habitats. Plants that come from sunny field situations—rudbeckias, for example—won't work.

Woodland is naturally easy to maintain. In such a setting, upkeep might be restricted to selective removal of unwanted vegetation: low-growing limbs, small trees, poison ivy, brambles, unwanted weeds, and large pieces of fallen wood. When this kind of competition is eliminated, the gardener can sit back and wait to see what happens. Delicate ferns, mosses, and fleeting wild flowers often will simply appear unexpectedly because soil and light conditions are perfect for their growth.

Arid-climate gardeners find suitable material among natives, cacti, succulents, and South African and Australian plants. Like the South African ice plant, drosanthemum, which has naturalized in California, these often have the added attraction of being fire retardant.

Nature abhors a vacuum: Bare ground swiftly sprouts a carpet of weeds. In the new garden it is kept covered by paving or planting. Bare spots are filled and the ground is kept covered—first by mulch, while plants are establishing themselves, and later by a cover of foliage. It should be remembered that it takes from two to three years for a planting of perennial ground cover to establish itself and fill out.

Selecting just the right plant for a particular spot will have a tremendous impact on the health and appearance of any garden and subsequently on the amount of maintenance involved. If a plant is well suited to its place in the garden, it thrives. It does what it is supposed to do and grows to its potential: Stems stretch up, leaves develop, flowers bloom. Beneath the ground a root system spreads out to nourish the plant. Such a plant outperforms weeds and survives the assaults of insects and diseases. The result is less work for the gardener.

A poorly placed plant—for example, a moisture lover in a dry spot—will grow slowly. Weeds will spring up all around it. Its poorly developed root system won't withstand drought; drooping foliage will send the gardener running for the watering can. A bad winter is all that is needed to deal the coup de grace. Sometimes people fall in love with a beautiful plant and insist on growing it even if conditions aren't right. It quickly becomes evident that the gardener must go to great lengths to mollycoddle an unsuitable plant if it is not to be stressed by an unsuitable microclimate. A stressed plant isn't beautiful and will never reach its potential. The sickly plant growing in the garden bears little relationship to the one that stole the gardener's heart.

In selecting plants for the new American garden, one has to consider first and foremost the garden site, the one thing that cannot change, and choose plants to suit that site. Each plant to be included must be carefully considered. Does it prefer shade or sun? Will it thrive in a moist or a dry soil? Will it survive the summer, the winter, or the dry season in a particular locale?

The second consideration is exactly what a plant requires in terms of upkeep to make the best possible appearance. Will it flop over if it isn't staked? How frequently will it need to be divided? Is it invasive—will it quickly crowd out less aggressive neighbors? After it blooms, are the withered flowers so big and unattractive that they have to be removed immediately? People who enjoy puttering in the garden often don't mind some of these chores. Others, who see the garden as a place in which to relax, find these chores overwhelming—or simply don't do them. For them, making selections from a more limited but reliable and fussless group of plants is the answer to having an attractive garden without spending endless hours each week maintaining it.

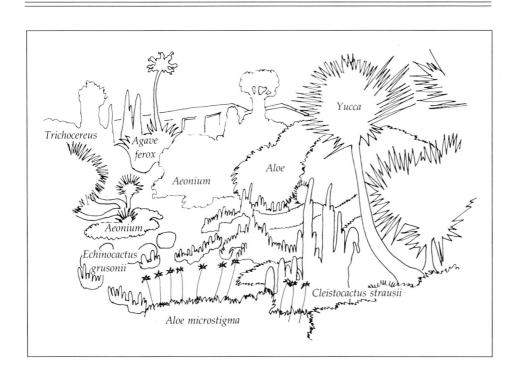

Plants from similar cultural niches will thrive with little outside help wherever conditions of the original habitat occur. This California garden featuring cacti and succulents needs no irrigation. At right foreground, a tall yucca grows from a ground cover of juniper. At left, orange-flowered *Aloe microstigma* mingles with silvery snowpole cactus *(Cleistocactus strausii)*. Round balls of golden barrel cactus *(Echinocactus grusonii)* and yellow-flowered aeonium serve as brightly colored ground cover. In the background are *Agave ferox* and the spires of *Trichocereus spachianus*.

The chapters on grasses, perennials, and plants with the right stuff concentrate on sturdy, undemanding, attractive herbaceous perennials. Used with discretion, they make adaptable ground cover. Other places to get ideas on what performs well in a given locale are local nurseries, botanical gardens, and neighbors' gardens.

More than anything else, gardeners have to educate their eyes to a new kind of garden, one that is suitable to their climate and is freer and more spontaneous. This means that plants must not be restricted to long borders surrounded by lawn, that landscaping can be something beyond grass and evergreen shrubs, that plants may be allowed to follow their life cycles out in the open: to bloom, and then to wither and die. It means that early spring is a time of open ground and swift development, that winter is a time of spare, stark beauty. Jens Jensen, a member of the Prairie school and a proponent of natural style landscaping, wrote:

> During winter the wind comes in crisp and invigorating from across the prairies. At this season of the year the landscape assumes a dreary look to many who do not see and cannot understand. But to others . . . the landscape sings a song of rich tonal beauty, a great prelude to dawn.

Training one's eyes to see beauty in all seasons obviates the need and taste for static green landscaping. In so doing, busywork is eliminated. While there is no such thing as a workless garden, the complexity and variety of the plantings in a well-designed garden are always a worthwhile trade-off for the amount of upkeep. Mindless, meaningless maintenance can be planned out of a garden before it is planted.

Keeping the ground covered—with paving, pools, plants, or mulch—is a good beginning. Eliminating high-maintenance plantings, such as lawn, and avoiding large trees and shrubs that change moisture and light conditions in the garden are the next steps. Instead of unmanageable giants, the use of easy-to-control, dynamic herbaceous material keeps the garden lively and in tune with the natural world. Choosing high-performance heroes of the plant world and planting them in the appropriate microclimates eliminate upkeep problems before they occur. Finally, training the eye to find beauty in all seasons is crucial. In the new garden, maintenance is kept to a meaningful minimum by careful advance planning.

Beauty is in the eye of the beholder. Providing an appealing view—even in winter—a pool is an alternate form of paving that serves as low-upkeep ground cover and an attractive view all year round. A submersible heater keeps this one from freezing.

Magnificent Ground Cover

GROUND COVERS ARE an attractive way to eliminate much of the busywork of garden maintenance. When people visit nurseries looking for ground covers, however, they are invariably shown plants that are spreading, evergreen, and under one foot tall. Once planted, such ground covers are neat and provide the gardener with areas that don't have to be mowed; they are also more interesting than landscaping that is only lawn and evergreen shrubbery. The only trouble is they remain virtually the same regardless of the season. The characteristics for which they were bred—uniformity and being evergreen—isolate these ground covers from the seasonal changes of the environment around them. In their static state, they lack excitement; they look artificial.

Yet there is no rule stating that ground covers have to be short, wide, and evergreen. And there is absolutely no reason in the world to confine the choice of lawn substitutes to those currently listed as "ground cover." Given the right location, any plant—whether thirty inches or six feet tall—can be used as ground cover. Ornamental grasses, black-eyed Susans, ferns, and showy sedums are only some of the many new candidates for ground cover. Well-chosen and well-situated perennial plants can move into a whole new role; they can become magnificent ground cover, responsive to the seasons, easy to care for, and wonderful to behold.

Why limit the garden to a few bland plants in the interest of custom

Maintenance is simplified when ground cover is well suited to climate. Golden barrel cactus (*Echinocactus grusonii*), and white torch cactus (*Cleistocactus morawetzianus*) are superb arid climate ground cover.

when the choices are truly astounding? Among the perennials and natives are thousands of candidates for dynamic, exciting, magnificent ground cover. Choice is governed only by personal taste, availability, and climate. Listed in this book is a much smaller group, selected for its reliability, versatility, and changing-year-round appearance.

Adventurous gardeners and those with special soil and climate requirements may need to look further afield. Each state, each county, each property has a different climate or microclimate. Only by matching the plant to its situation will it reach its potential.

Karl Foerster described "class heroes" as those members of a class of plants that stand head and shoulders above the rest. Not the rank and file, these are the ones with the right stuff: They are not fussy about location, are good looking at all stages of their development, are freely blooming, noninvasive, and remain upright without staking. In the new garden, where only a few plants are chosen for mass plantings, it is crucial to choose "heroes." Only an outstanding individual does the job and continues to shine, no matter what the season.

Perennials are herbaceous plants whose active growth phase takes place within a given growing season. Roots stay alive from year to year and send up a great new rush of growth when the time is right. When they emerge from the ground in spring, perennials seem to do so at a given signal, appearing overnight in an otherwise naked landscape. Suddenly the entire earth awakens and signs of life are everywhere. Once started, the growth of perennials is prodigious. There is tension and excitement in their great rush of growth. Each day brings a new development—a new leaf, a swelling bud, an uncurling flower.

Growth accelerates until midsummer, when flowers bloom in abundance and the garden is as full as it can be. Summer brings a different mood to the garden. The volume of plants in foliage and flower is at its peak. For a few weeks the garden rests, satisfied, luxuriating in its fullness.

Sometime in late summer, nature gives another signal and, one by one, the plants fall into line. They begin to color, to wither, to recede. Where there were flowers, seeds form. What was a deep rich green turns burgundy or gold or yellow. Again there is a sense of tension, but instead of the quickening rush that was spring, these changes are slow, lingering, and reluctant. The first frost transforms the landscape. Shapes become spare and brittle; rusts and shades of wheat replace the green.

With magnificent ground cover, sensitive to the seasons, it is possible to determine the time of year by simply looking at the plants. When they are massed, the seasonal statement they make is all the more eloquent because the dynamics of a single plant's emergence, maturity, and demise are multiplied. What is small and fragile and fleeting becomes an eye-stopping spectacle when multiplied by dozens or even

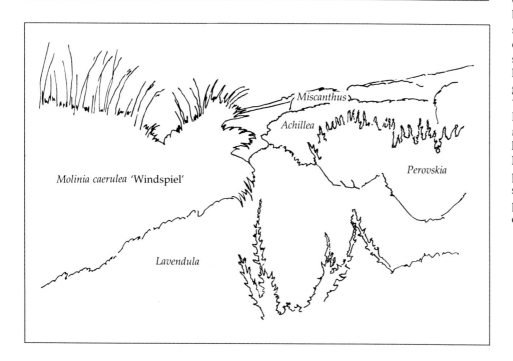

Ground cover doesn't have to be low and evergreen. The seemingly random repetition of perennials—here, Russian sage *(Perovskia atriplicifolia)*, lavender, tall purple moor grass *(Molinea caerulea altissima* 'Windspiel'), achilleas, and Eulalia grass *(Miscanthus sinensis)*—imparts a meadow look to this seaside garden. Massing plants brings the planting up to landscape scale, while interspersing plants of different heights and colors avoids monotony.

Masses of perennials and ornamental grasses convey the message of the seasons. In full summer the garden is voluptuous. Herbaceous plants, fountain grass (*Pennisetum alopecuroides*), and 'Goldsturm' rudbeckias are as lush and full as they can be. Witch hazel, the small tree, and bergenia, in right foreground, bloomed in spring along with masses of bulbs for early season display. 'Autumn Joy' sedums, left foreground, have just begun their long, late season of show.

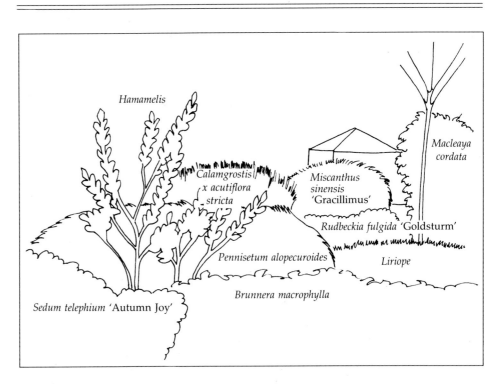

Hamamelis

Calamgrostis x acutiflora stricta

Miscanthus sinensis 'Gracillimus'

Macleaya cordata

Rudbeckia fulgida 'Goldsturm'

Pennisetum alopecuroides

Liriope

Brunnera macrophylla

Sedum telephium 'Autumn Joy'

hundreds. In a traditional perennial border, the progress of a single plant's development is a quiet mystery being played out in small pockets next to the shrubbery. In the new garden, masses of magnificent perennial ground cover magnify the drama of growth and development—of life itself—to a scale that is noticeable in the landscape at large.

A single unfurling fern, a lacy unfolding astilbe are some of nature's small wonders; two dozen ferns unfolding among blooming daffodils says spring in a way that is not forgotten. Fifty lacy astilbes unfolding makes for exciting, dynamic ground cover that promises more and better to come. Masses of perennials make a profound impact in the landscape. No group is static; color, height, and volume are always changing. The entire landscape becomes dynamic—moving and changing as the seasons progress.

No longer is the garden an artificial island of static green in the environment. Using masses of herbaceous material ties the garden to its surroundings. No longer isolated and artificial, it celebrates the seasons with the landscape around it.

Perennials were traditionally used in special borders, where they were combined for summer show. The art of the border was arranging small groups of perennials to give a continual sequence of bloom in which color and height were coordinated. While an entire landscape composed of such combinations is possible, it demands an enormous investment in planning and upkeep. The great danger of using the numbers and varieties of plants of a traditional perennial border is a motley effect, with too many plants of too many colors grouped in twos and threes.

Massing plants gives a more formal effect that is better suited to landscape use; the eye can take in sweeps of a single type of plant easily but is irritated by too many small distractions. Massing combines the best of gardening and landscaping. The excitement of emerging plants that grow rapidly and bloom is here. So are the large-scale effects. When massed, each stage of the perennial's life becomes a landscape feature. Thousands of emerging rudbeckia leaves or bright green tufts of sedum serve as moving, changing ground cover.

Although periods of massed bloom in the new garden are spectacular, the in-between times have their own rich beauty, too. Never before has texture been such an important element of garden and landscape. Grasses of soft, dusty green, the rosy-tinted, leathery leaves of bergenias, the matte green of brunneras enliven the garden with vibrant and changing patterns and colors. The secret of their powerful effect is massing. In ones, twos, and threes these plants have interesting foliage; in tens, twenties, and thirties they carpet the garden with magnificent texture.

Maintenance is simplified both by the absence of lawn and the fact that each plant in a given mass of ground cover is identical. Weeds and unwanted plants are easy to spot and remove, and the entire area has the same light and water requirements.

A ground cover of perennials, evergreens, and ornamental grasses adds subtle color and texture to this late-December landscape. Frost turns bergenia to shades of rose and maroon. Deep green yews contrast with winter-blanched maiden grass (*Miscanthus sinensis* 'Gracillimus').

Massing of perennial plants brings the garden up to landscape scale. *Astilbe* 'Fanal' and *A.* 'Red Sentinel,' bright green epimedium, *Liriope spicata,* and palm sedge *(Carex muskingumensis)* offer an exciting, colorful, and textured alternative to lawn that adds easy maintenance into the bargain.

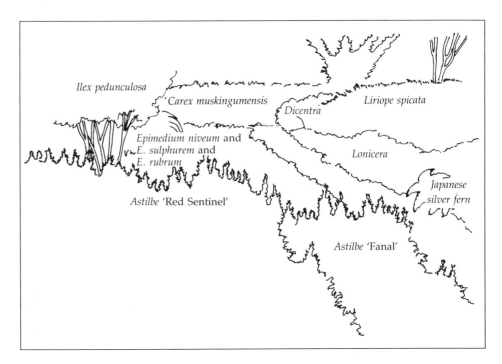

Ilex pedunculosa

Carex muskingumensis

Dicentra

Liriope spicata

Epimedium niveum and *E. sulphurem* and *E. rubrum*

Lonicera

Astilbe 'Red Sentinel'

Japanese silver fern

Astilbe 'Fanal'

Of course, careful thought has to go into siting masses of plants in the first place. The placement of each mass of perennials should be directly related to the microclimatic factors in a particular yard. Shady areas under trees will support shade-loving perennials; a windy, exposed spot next to a driveway demands another kind of plant. Dry, sunny places make good homes for Mediterranean plants. Segmenting a property into specific climatic zones such as dry sun, dry shade, moist shade, or moist sun simplifies the job of placing the masses.

Each piece of land has a vegetative history and will often revert to an earlier stage with very little effort. In some parts of the Northeast, unmown meadows will revert to forests in three years or less. In the Southwest, any vegetation that is not indigenous or hailing from a similar climate requires constant irrigation in the dry season. Fighting nature is an unending uphill struggle demanding constant maintenance; gardeners can simplify, beautify, and save money by making the best of what they already have.

Instead of battling shade or liming an acid woodland in a hopeless struggle for grass, a home owner can maximize the positive features of his lot by growing what he alone can grow: a field of wild flowers, a moss lawn, a ground cover of ferns. In an arid zone, a garden of aloes, cacti, and agaves is both beautifully appropriate and unique to its area. On the sea coast, where wind and salt spray are damaging to many plants, native dune grasses and succulents look good and work well. One of the most nostalgic and beautiful new trends in American gardening is the meadow garden—or, in its midwestern form, the prairie. In both, mixtures of grasses and wild flowers mingle in a high ground cover that changes color each time a group of plants within the meadow blooms. In winter, grasses blanch with the frost; seed pods in earthen tones provide texture for the gardener and food for wildlife.

There are several approaches to establishing a meadow. One can buy seed, sow it, and hope that it germinates before the seeds already present on the ground do. Another method is simply allowing the plants in a field to grow up, then selectively removing unwanted species. A third approach—the most surefire—is also the most expensive. It involves placing well-developed wild flower and grass plants in the random patterns observed in nature. A variation on this approach is the establishment of a stylized meadow, using reliable garden plants. Of course, one can also use the best combination of the other approaches. More information on meadows can be found later in this chapter.

Sometimes what seems to be an enormous drawback becomes the garden's most important feature. Land that doesn't drain enough to support lawn or conventional plants will support bog plants. A yard with a rock outcropping makes a stunning rock garden. A lot that has terrible soil, builder's fill perhaps, might be paved or decked, leaving only small areas for planting. Any garden should fit into what is already on the land—not the other way around. The inspiration for the garden must come from the land and not from convention.

No single garden can have it all. A little garden of timid conventionality—a little lawn, a little patio, a little bed of a dozen flowers—cancels itself out aesthetically. Especially in small-space gardens, bold decisions on a few strong features make all the difference. Big masses of a few excellent perennials will actually make the garden look larger and will simplify maintenance. Bold masses of magnificent ground cover will capture the excitement and seasonal dynamics of the garden on a scale that suits the landscape.

MEADOWS AND PRAIRIES

In recent years, meadows and prairies have gained increasing popularity as interesting, low-maintenance ground cover. Both are composed of a community of native plants that forms high, herbaceous ground cover in an open, sunny place. Naturally occurring meadows were large clearings in forested land in the Northeast and Northwest; prairies, vast expanses of grasslands, were the dominant vegetation of the Great Plains.

Recreating an authentic prairie or meadow composed of only native plants takes a knowledge of native plants and some effort. Ideal maintenance for prairies, for example, is periodic burning to destroy woody plants. Some gardeners enjoy carrying out the details of such authentic prairie maintenance. Those who live in areas with "no burn" ordinances must rely on periodic mowing to take the place of burning. It is also possible to install a planting with a meadow or prairie look. There are several approaches, and choice is a matter of personal taste.

A meadow from seed

Many seed companies, as well as native plant and prairie restoration groups, offer seed. Preparing the ground before sowing seeds is crucial. First, sod must be removed. For very large areas experts favor turning up the ground several times; this allows existing seeds in the plot to germinate so that plant competition can be destroyed before the meadow mix is sown. As soon as a new crop of unwanted seedlings covers the ground, but before it has grown large enough to make shallow tilling difficult, it is turned under. One might opt to do this two or three times before planting, or even every three weeks for an entire growing season, to give the seeds of meadow flowers a good start.

Once the meadow is planted, watering is crucial. Newly planted seeds and young plants need supplemental watering until they are established.

Steve Davis of the American Horticultural Society at River Farm in Mount Vernon, Virginia, offers the following advice for starting and maintaining a meadow from seed. Having learned the hard way not to deep till—tilling brought up six acres of pokeweed seeds that had lain dormant for a century—Davis recommends just roughing the soil surface before casting the seed. For a small area he suggests merely raking to loosen the topsoil. The amount of seed sown is crucial. If it is too

This meadow at River Farm, home of the American Horticultural Society, was started from seed. After May-blooming daisies, black-eyed Susans dominate in June. The meadow changes constantly as new plant communities develop, bloom, and go to seed.

A meadow at the National Arboretum in Washington, D.C., was created by simply allowing a field to grow. Nature provides a delightful series of blooming plant communities beginning in late spring with plants like daisies. Here, swamp milkweed blooms in August to be followed by heleniums, goldenrods, and asters. Left to stand over winter, the meadow turns to wheats and taupes, providing form, beauty, and a haven for wildlife. Maintenance consists of yearly mowing and selectively cutting out undesirable weeds and trees.

Looking like a field of golden wheat, a meadow of fountain grass *(Pennisetum alopecuroides)* glows in the autumn sunshine. Creating a meadow by installing plants at the correct intervals for optimum growth is more expensive than starting one from seed but allows the gardener to exercise complete control over what is grown. Fountain grass, attractive throughout the winter, should be cut back in late February before new growth begins.
(Photo by Monika Burwell)

much, a splash of early annuals in the seed mixture will crowd out other plants that take longer to develop. If it is too little the number of species may diminish as showy annuals give way to deeply rooted perennials. For the meadow at River Farm, Davis feels that two pounds of seed per acre is optimum. He recommends reseeding every two years, which he likens to applying a "top dressing." The meadow is mowed once each year in the early spring.

A meadow from a field

Cole Burrell of the National Arboretum in Washington, D.C., used another approach to establish a two-acre meadow there: He simply let a field grow. Undesirable plants, such as seedling trees, honeysuckle, weedy panicums, and ragweeds, are systematically pulled or cut out. Each year, as more desirable species gain ground, the number of plants to be destroyed diminishes. Ragweed and other species that require sunlight and bare ground in order to germinate are shaded out. Some desirable plants have been "plugged in" (planted as established seedlings) as well. Burrell favors allowing the meadow to stand over the winter, both for its attractive appearance and for the cover it supplies for wildlife (a covey of quail has made its home in the arboretum's meadow). Mowing is done in earliest spring.

In a stylized meadow the number of species used—whether seeded or plugged in—is carefully controlled. One advantage to this method is that desirable plants are clearly recognizable to even a novice gardener, thus simplifying weed control. Being able to use outstanding hybrids as meadow flowers is another advantage. A few suitable ones from among many are the medium-sized *Achillea filipendulina* 'Coronation Gold,' daylilies, and *Centaurea* 'John Coutts.' Color can also be controlled in a stylized meadow. Many combinations of yellows and golds, mauves, pinks, and white are possible. *Lythrum* 'Morden's Pink,' *Echinacea* 'Bressingham Hybrids,' astrantia, and asters combine in shades of mauve and pink.

Medium-sized ornamental grasses are excellent subjects for a stylized meadow. Good choices are fountain grass *(Pennisetum alopecuroides)*; switch grass *(Panicum virgatum)*, a prairie grass; and the cultivar, *P. virgatum* 'Rotstrahlbusch,' which forms red clouds of seeds. Grasses, which constitute a large percentage of material in both natural meadows and prairies, are especially attractive in winter.

A person not completely sold on a meadow might opt for a mass planting of annuals before investing money and effort in a perennial planting. Annual grasses, cosmos, strawflowers, black-eyed Susans, and coreopsis might be some of the plants included.

The stylized meadow, with its masses of the same or very carefully blended groups of plants, has a more formal look. In communities with weed control ordinances, this might be the meadow-propagating method of choice. Basically, plants are either seeded and thinned or planted at intervals that allow for ground cover without crowding. In order to enjoy them throughout the winter, owners of stylized meadows cut them back in very early spring, before new growth begins.

A stylized meadow

Masses of nasturtiums, an annual plant, are a temporary ground cover around fig trees in the courtyard of this southern California home. Once the plants have been thinned, care is limited to irrigation.
(Photo by Joe Holly)

Plants
with Presence

MASSING PERENNIALS as meadow and magnificent ground cover brings small plants up to a scale that makes a statement in the landscape. Some plants, however, do not require repetition to be noticed. Size, color, and habit endow certain plants with personas that are impossible to overlook. These plants dominate a garden space. They have presence.

Used singly or in very small groups, the bold shapes, colors, and sizes of plants with presence have an impact on the landscape scale. Their height and shape punctuate large masses of lower-growing perennials, providing contrast and a sense of depth. Especially in very small gardens, where a collection of very small plants in the same spot would quickly reveal the garden's paltry dimensions, massive plants evoke a sense of grandeur.

Evocative of something far larger than an individual property, plants with presence belong in the new garden. They conjure up nature on the grand scale—suggesting the majesty of tundra or desert, forest or field. Each one is an imposing representative of the larger environment.

A perennial plant with presence starts anew each spring from the roots and grows into a pristine plant with fresh new stems and fresh new leaves. As such an individual reaches its enormous proportions, the actual process of growth is a drama by itself—a garden feature. When played against the performance of bulbs and the development of masses

A quietly green, small grass all summer, purpurescens silver grass (*Miscanthus purpurescens*) is catapulted into the limelight in the fall when its foliage turns bright red-orange. Growing here in a bed of rockspray (cotoneaster), purpurescens silver grass is backed by fountain grass (*Pennisetum alopecuroides*) in winter coloring.

of ground cover and other more quickly maturing individuals, the ponderous growth of a massive specimen builds suspense and adds movement to the garden.

By summer, when the plant's full stature has been achieved, a plant with presence is impressive in the luxuriance of its foliage. There is a rich lushness always at or slightly below eye level, where it can be enjoyed, not a canopy far above the garden that profoundly affects conditions below but cannot be seen. Accessibility is an important aspect of a plant with presence. It is one of nature's wonders—amazing in size, shape, and color, but never out of reach.

Large grasses have magnetic presence once they reach their full growth. Their immense volume dramatically alters the garden's space so that its summer appearance is ripe and full to bursting. Grasses' long, soft blades catch even the slightest of breezes and flutter and sway, adding both movement and sound to the garden. Many grasses are late bloomers, sporting pink to white plumes in autumn when the rest of the garden has already begun the melancholy and reluctant passage into winter. After frost they turn brilliant shades of almond and wheat, as striking in the winter landscape as flower colors are against summer greens. Grouping a giant grass with other frost-touched material, such as *Sedum*

A native live oak dominated this California property long before the house was built. Beneath the oak, a cluster of rugged rocks counterbalances enormous limbs.

telephium 'Autumn Joy' or the chocolate seed pods of *Rudbeckia fulgida* 'Goldsturm,' creates a larger-than-life dried-flower bouquet for winter viewing.

Virtually all grasses that have been blanched by frost or drought have presence. California's nickname, the Golden State, derives from the golden color of its grasses in the dry season. In the East, grasses glowing golden in the gray winter days seem to be repositories of summer sunlight. Blanched grasses bring life and contrast to evergreen plantings.

Because of their size, plants with presence often form the framework against which other plants are sited. They provide structure and stability in a planting. One such grouping in a small garden becomes an ever-changing tableaux during the growing season and a striking focus throughout the winter. Plants with presence in larger gardens tie a garden together or lead the eye in the desired direction. Some, like the plume poppy *(Macleaya cordata)*, have unique foliage that sets them apart from their neighbors. Others, like the giant grasses, have a neutralizing effect on other plants. Subtle, dusty green leaves like those of *Miscanthus sinensis* 'Gracillimus' serve to mediate between vibrant colors and textures, bringing greater harmony to a planting.

Other plants have personas because of unique coloring. Among these is the *Miscanthus sinensis zebrinus strictus*, a striking bright green and

The century plant *(Agave americana)* is a symbol of the Southwest. With its glaucous coloring, distinctive shape, and huge size, it is impressive wherever it can be grown. Gardeners in arid, frost-free areas may choose from a wealth of unusual succulents, agaves, and cacti to create carefree gardens of great presence.

Edging a swimming pool, lush maiden grass (*Miscanthus sinensis* 'Gracillimus'), fountain grass *(Pennisetum alopecuroides)*, and *Hibiscus palustris* command attention. The fine, cascading foliage of the grasses contrasts with hibiscus's toothed, heart-shaped leaf.

yellow striped giant with such a strong personality that its companions must be chosen with care. Yellow-flowered masses and the matte gray-green of achillea harmonize beautifully. The sulphur yellow form of *Coreopsis verticillata* is another companion. Deep purple on the underside of its rounded leaf, *Ligularia dentata* 'Othello' is an eye-catching, relatively small-sized plant that will bestow a sense of place on even the most forlorn and undistinguished garden corner.

Some plants derive their presence not from size but from shape. In tight garden spots that would not support a larger plant, an individual with striking foliage and an interesting shape enlivens without overwhelming. Adam's needle *(Yucca filamentosa)*, an evergreen hummock of blue-green spikes, Spanish bayonet *(Yucca aloifolia)*, and a semi-evergreen sedge *(Carex pendula)*, with its gracefully arching seed heads, are among the latter.

Cacti, aloes with distinctive shapes and textures, have enormous presence. Unlike herbaceous perennials, which grow rapidly, cacti's growth is imperceptible. Because of their slow growth and unusual shapes they may be combined into a living "still life" to grace a dooryard. For gardens in areas of low or seasonal rainfall, cacti provide unique, care-free, and distinctive landscaping that makes few demands on resources or time.

Cascading ribbonlike foliage of giant miscanthus *(Miscanthus floridulus)* grows to eight or nine feet in a period of three months. Although it prefers sun, giant miscanthus will make slow, steady progress in light shade.

Using plants with presence makes it easy to predict what the garden will look like in three, five, or ten years. Although they are frequently quite large, these plants function as ordinary perennials once allotted space and resources. Unlike trees and many shrubs, they will not continually alter shade patterns and the water available to neighboring plants as they mature. Though massive, these perennials never outgrow their spots. Because their great bulk is at or below eye level where it is most impressive, they never overwhelm but simply reach a fixed height and stop—no matter how old they are. In contrast to trees and shrubs, they are easy to control and require no pruning.

Compared to typical garden center offerings—the tiny arborvitae that may quickly obscure the front door or the cute little white pine that may take over the front lawn—plants with presence are well-behaved giants. Their size is predictable, their growth is containable. They impress and delight but do not overwhelm. Plants with presence are hardworking; while they delight and amaze, they serve as screening, as a framework for other plants, and as sculpture. They relieve the horizontal monotony that comes with mass plantings. These powerful individuals are used singly and in very small groups so that they are effective without becoming too much of a good thing.

Green and preparing to flower in the dry California summer, an opuntia and a neighboring aloe have shapes with great presence. Even in harsh sunlight, dense, distinctly shaped foliage casts deep shadows. On the horizon is a row of Monterrey pines (*Pinus radiata*).

Mounding maiden grass (*Miscanthus sinensis* 'Gracillimus') exhibits a powerful persona rising from a bed of bergenia, glistening in the June sunshine.

PLANTS WITH PRESENCE

Tall, sculptural plants

The giant reed *(Arundo donax)* has nothing if not presence. Growing reliably to fifteen feet, it will attain twenty feet in excellent conditions. Except in very old, established clumps, giant reed has the open, airy, sculptural look of a thin stand of giant bamboo. Gardeners in the far South might substitute the banana for the giant reed. In the Southwest and southern California, tall cacti, the ocotillo plant, or yucca might serve as sculptural material. Tall plants with persona enhance the size of a small garden and add drama. Used in the foreground, they force perspective. In the background they are especially effective at breaking up a solid expanse of fence or wall. Used in conjunction with other, low-growing material, tall sculptural plants anchor a planting, providing framework and accentuating it as a focal point.

Giant perennials

Wondrous giant perennials serve as focal points, relieving uniform masses with their bold presence. Plume poppy *(Macleaya cordata)* is a giant perennial with a strong personality. Growing six to eight feet tall, the plume poppy's neatly cut rounded leaves overlap shingle-fashion around multiple stalks. Pale pinky buff–colored plumes bloom in July. Bluestem Joe Pye weed *(Eupatorium purpureum)* blooms in late August on eight-foot stalks. Cow-parsnip *(Heracleum mantegazzianum)*—which generates an allergic reaction in some people—has immense, deeply cut leaves and large flower umbels in midsummer that turn to sculptural seed heads later on. Moisture loving *Gunnera manicata,* with its umbrella-sized leaves and wide, spreading habit, is an eye-stopping garden showpiece.

Virtually all grasses of the genus miscanthus have enormous presence by virtue of their dense, luxuriant mounds of foliage. Excellent for screening, miscanthus grasses next to a paved area or a pool provide wonderful contrast in the rich density of their foliage. They extend a garden visually by suggesting limitless space. For this reason they are a fine choice—where there is enough sun—for the small garden. After frost, their winter color provides a second, more striking season of show. All prefer sun and, with the exception of the cultivars *M. sinensis* 'Silberfeder' and *M. sinensis variegatus,* are hardy to zone 4.

'Silberfeder' is hardy to zone 5 and *Miscanthus sinesis variegatus,* which requires shade, is hardy to zone 5–6.

Giant *Miscanthus floridulus* is the tallest and the most upright, growing to eight feet. Useful as a screen, it carries the bulk of its foliage at three feet or higher. For this reason it is best planted among tall perennials to camouflage its bareness below the knees.

Eulalia grass *(M. sinensis),* growing to seven feet with plumes, makes a good screen as well as a natural-looking specimen. The cultivar 'Gracillimus'—the most refined and gardenesque in leaf and habit—has narrow, darker green blades with a white rib and grows to a very dense, cascading vase shape. *M. sinensis condensatus,* growing to six feet, is a good compromise between the other two.

Dense foliage plants

Unexpected color in the landscape demands attention. The light, bright green of the clump bamboo *(Sinarundinaria nitida),* the oily liver purple of *Ligularia dentata* 'Othello,' the glowing autumn orange of purpurescens silver grass *(Miscanthus purpurescens)* all have presence and stand out from the greens around them. Some of these colorful individuals are powerful all by themselves—among them, zebra or porcupine grasses *(M. sinensis zebrinus* and *zebrinus strictus).* Some, like the intense glowing red Japanese blood grass *Imperata cylindrica rubra* 'Red Baron,' have presence only in large masses. Switch grass *(Panicum virgatum)* is another plant that requires multiplication to achieve its powerful winter presence.

PLANTS WITH STRIKING COLOR

Plants with unusual forms are at their best in a spare landscape. Winter in a temperate climate and summer in an arid one are times when bright light and deep shadow accentuate the forms of yucca, aloes, and cacti. *Yucca filamentosa* (zones 5 to 9) and the smaller *Yucca glauca* (zones 4 to 9) don't need a warm, dry climate to survive. Several grasses have unusual forms; among them are blue oat grass *(Helictotrichon sempervirens),* a two-foot mound of spiky blue-green foliage, and drooping sedge *(Carex pendula),* which grows to three feet and has an arching flower and seed stalks.

PLANTS WITH UNUSUAL FORMS

C H A P T E R

7

Ornamental

Grasses

"MOTHER EARTH'S HAIR" was what German nursery-man Karl Foerster called the ornamental grasses that he championed for garden use. He thought that grasses were too basic a part of every landscape and too important a part of the earth's vegetation to be omitted from gardens. Over the entire earth, grasses are certainly the most familiar and ubiquitous of all plant forms. Because of their role in the natural landscape, because of their flowing, graceful beauty, and because of their adaptability, ornamental grasses play an important role in the new garden.

Although lawn grasses have long been an element of American gardens, in the new garden, new grasses—giants and miniatures, evergreens and variegated forms—appear on their own terms. Unmowed, untrimmed, they assume natural forms as loose, flowing mounds and bristling hummocks. Grown this way, they imbue the garden with a wild, natural look that is evocative of prairie and field. But it is not only for their loose, flowing shapes that ornamental grasses are excellent choices for the new garden. Their dynamic growth and changing seasonal appearance, as well as their low maintenance needs, make them ideal candidates for inclusion.

Few grasses are effective in spring. Their rapid and vigorous growth, however, dovetails with tulip bloom and the flowering of early perennials. In summer, ornamental grasses come into their own. They attain

A dried bouquet of frost-touched material includes, clockwise from left bottom: the seed heads of *Rudbeckia fulgida* 'Goldsturm,' seed heads of *Calamagrostis x acutiflora stricta, Pennisetum alopecuroides,* and *Miscanthus purpurescens.*

full height and great volume, dramatically altering space in a garden. When large grasses are used, the raw, wide-open look of early spring swiftly changes to lush density. As a group, grasses are late bloomers. Their flowers appear in late summer and early fall, when other perennials are finished flowering. They are tremendously useful in extending the blooming season.

Care of ornamental grasses is simple. Most respond to the same fertilizer used for ordinary garden perennials. A few, among them the fescues, do better in soils of low fertility. Because of their attractive winter appearance, when foliage turns to pale wheat and almond colors, grasses are cut back once each year in late February or early March before new growth begins. Care of individual grasses will be discussed in the section that follows.

For Americans, the new garden with its ornamental grasses strikes a familiar and nostalgic chord. For many, it enfolds actual memories of childhood alongside sunny fields. For others, it is only slightly removed from daily experience: the landscape seen through the car window or on vacation in the country. Norman Rockwell suggested it and Andrew Wyeth painted it. Generations of schoolchildren sang about the landscape that is "over the river and through the woods," of "amber fields of grain." Reminiscent to all, it is a landscape of the heart.

ORNAMENTAL GRASSES

Giant-sized

Arundo donax (Giant Reed): The giant reed will grow reliably to fifteen feet and, with ample warmth and moisture, up to twenty feet. It tolerates moist soil during the growing season but does well in ordinary garden soil. Although the giant reed, a native of Europe, south of the Alps, is hardy in zone 5, it is one of the few grasses that does best with some winter protection. It requires a position in full sun with good drainage—especially in winter. The giant reed makes a tall, striking bamboolike sculptural specimen and an airy screen that turns to bright almond after frost. Only older, well-established clumps are dense enough to serve as total screening. Giant reeds should be cut back to ten inches whenever the gardener finds time after December, by which time wind damage will have diminished its winter appeal. The giant reed is propagated by division.

Cortaderia selloana (Pampas Grass): Pampas grass, hardy in zones 8 through 10 and in various places farther north, is a striking four-foot mound of foliage that bears immense white plumes on stalks that can reach twelve feet. Pampas grass requires full sun and good drainage—especially in winter. Gardeners in more northerly climates who wish to grow this native of the Argentine pampas may resort to containers. Otherwise, ravenna grass, with a similar habit, is a hardy substitute.

Miscanthus floridulus (Giant Miscanthus): Giant miscanthus is a foot tall in mid-May and reaches chest high by June, generally growing to eight feet by August. Its broad blades are a medium to deep green and

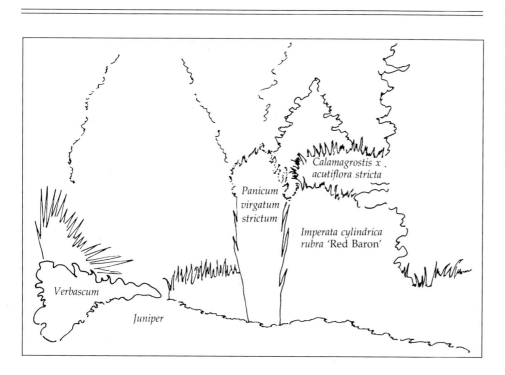

Behind a ground cover of prostrate juniper and an upright form of switch grass (*Panicum virgatum strictum*), a field of Japanese blood grass (*Imperata cylindrica rubra* 'Red Baron') glows in a September garden. Visible in the background is feather reed grass (*Calamagrostis x acutiflora stricta*).

At the Limerock Ornamental Grass Nursery in Port Matilda, Pennsylvania, only the finest varieties of grasses are grown. From left to right, rows of grasses are maiden grass (*Miscanthus sinensis* 'Gracillimus'), the long, medium green, very uniform row; and prairie cord grass (*Spartina pectinata aureo-marginata*), the bright green, short row in left foreground. *Miscanthus sinensis condensatus*, blooming deep red, follows the spartina. At right are three rows of *Calamagrostis x acutiflora stricta*.

An easy to maintain oval of lawn sets off a collection of ornamental grasses. From left are *Miscanthus sinensis* 'Autumn Light,' described by its owner as a "perfect grass that never does anything bad," purple moor grass *(Molinia caerulea)* behind a patch of 'Big Blue' liriope, and the Korean calamagrostis *(C. arundinacea brachytricha),* with its showy foxtail blooms in October. Under the tree in the center of the lawn is shade-tolerant *Spodiopogon sibiricus.* In the background, a row of fountain grass *(Pennisetum alopecuroides)* backed by maiden grass *(Miscanthus sinensis* 'Gracillimus') edges the lawn.

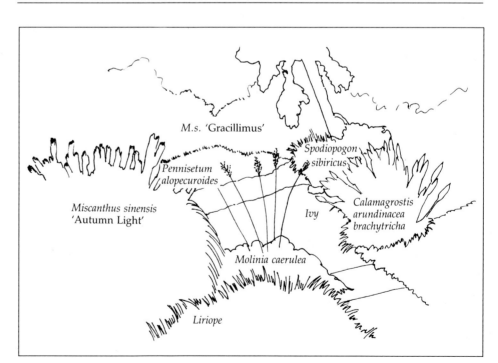

M.s. 'Gracillimus'

Spodiopogon sibiricus

Pennisetum alopecuroides

Miscanthus sinensis 'Autumn Light'

Ivy

Calamagrostis arundinacea brachytricha

Molinia caerulea

Liriope

give a dense, tropical appearance to a planting. It will grow tall and thick faster when located in moist sun but makes slow, steady progress even in full shade. Because a clump tends to be thinner "below the knees," giant miscanthus looks best when planted behind large perennials like daylilies or kniphofias. Giant miscanthus is the last miscanthus to bloom in September. It turns peach-colored with the first few frosts, then gradually blanches to almond; it is effective until around January, by which time the wind will have diminished its appeal. Giant miscanthus comes from China and Japan and is hardy to zone 4. Propagation is by division.

Miscanthus sinensis (Eulalia Grass): Eulalia grass forms a dense seven-foot clump of cascading foliage that is splendid as a specimen and very effective as a screen from June until February. The foliage of Eulalia grass in summer color and texture is reason enough to grow the plant. Eulalia grass, hardy to zone 4, has a broader spreading growth habit and coarser foliage than maiden grass; it grows in a characteristic ring, with the center dying out as the crown diameter increases. In mid-August, silky fan-shaped inflorescences open red, turning to white with age. After frost, they curl into feathery white plumes that remain attractive throughout the winter, when foliage turns to a spectacular almond color. Eulalia grass is cut back to six or eight inches each February. It is robust enough to be burned back, where ordinances allow. Eulalia grass is propagated by division.

Miscanthus sinensis 'Gracillimus' (Maiden Grass): Maiden grass, 'Gracillimus,' a cultivar of Eulalia grass with finer, darker, narrower white-ribbed blades, is hardy to zone 4. It is smaller, growing to only five feet, and more compact, forming with age a dense vase shape that is generally more refined and gardenesque than that of Eulalia grass. Flowering is also later (mid-September) and may not occur in northern areas with short growing seasons. Even without the flowers, which are most attractive in winter, the foliage serves as an excellent garden foil in summer when maiden grass's mound of shifting, whispering foliage acts as a mediator between blocks of colored perennials. After frost, maiden grass contrasts superbly with the deep green of evergreen shrubs and trees. Propagation is by division.

Miscanthus sinensis 'Silberfeder' (Silverfeather Grass): Silverfeather grass is similar to Eulalia in medium green foliage and form, but it is somewhat finer and blooms reliably and much earlier, with large, attractive silvery white plumes at the end of July or the beginning of August. Hardy to zone 5, it is the first among the large miscanthus grasses to bloom. Propagate by division.

Miscanthus sinensis condensatus (Condensatus): Condensatus grows to a dense, five- to six-foot-tall clump of somewhat less compact habit (the way a plant is shaped) than 'Gracillimus,' with broad, flat, white-ribbed blades, hardy to zone 4–5. Effective from June until late February when it is cut back to six inches, it flowers reliably in late August to early

September. Inflorescences open burgundy, turning to bronze. Propagation is by division.

Miscanthus sinensis variegatus; Miscanthus sinensis zebrinus (Zebra Grass); *Miscanthus sinensis zebrinus strictus* (Porcupine Grass): The variegated forms of Eulalia grass are somewhat smaller than the species, growing to a broad vase shape only slightly over four feet. Variegatus, which has white and green longitudinal striping, is also somewhat more tender (hardy to zone 5–6) and requires part shade. Zebra grass is bright green with yellow horizontal bands. Porcupine grass is similar in coloring to zebra grass but is narrower and more stiffly upright. Both zebra and porcupine grass are hardy to zone 5. Because of their distinctive coloring, they must be used with discretion. Both make excellent companions to yellow flowers, such as achilleas and yellow coreopsis.

Erianthus ravennae (Ravenna Grass): Ravenna grass is the northern substitute for pampas grass *(Cortaderia selloana).* It is a striking specimen in flower and after frost. Its showy, long plumes, appearing in late August, are held high above the three-foot bushy plants, swaying and shining white. In some years, tall flower stalks form, but the flowers do not fully extend—possibly the result of overly cold soil. Ravenna grass requires light, well-drained soil. In cold, wet clay soils, it may not flower at all. For this reason gardeners in clay soil areas grow ravenna grass on a mound to ensure perfect drainage. Ravenna grass is a powerful, attention-demanding specimen *after* the long flower stalks have formed. It is effective from August until it is cut back in late February. It is propagated by seed or division.

Medium-sized

Carex pendula (Drooping Sedge): Drooping sedge, hardy to zone 6, is a bright yellowish green evergreen mound of gracefully arching, leathery, straplike foliage, with striking inflorescences that arch high over the plant in May and June. It requires careful placement in shade, with protection from drying winds and winter sun. Drooping sedge also needs room for its arching inflorescences to be seen to best advantage. It looks good when planted with low ground cover such as epimedium or small palm sedge.

Calamagrostis x acutiflora stricta (Feather Reed Grass): Feather reed grass, hardy to zone 5 and areas farther north with adequate snow cover, is a robust-growing grass with extremely showy flower plumes that develop into striking, very erect, wheat-colored seed heads. Plumes appear in June and later turn to seeds that remain on the plant well into winter when its basal foliage has an attractive yellow cast. The entire plant, measuring five feet with seed heads, is of upright habit and provides a distinctly vertical accent in the garden that is effective from June until late February when it is cut back. It requires a position in full sun. Propagation is by division.

Calamagrostis arundinacea brachytricha (Korean Reed Grass): From June

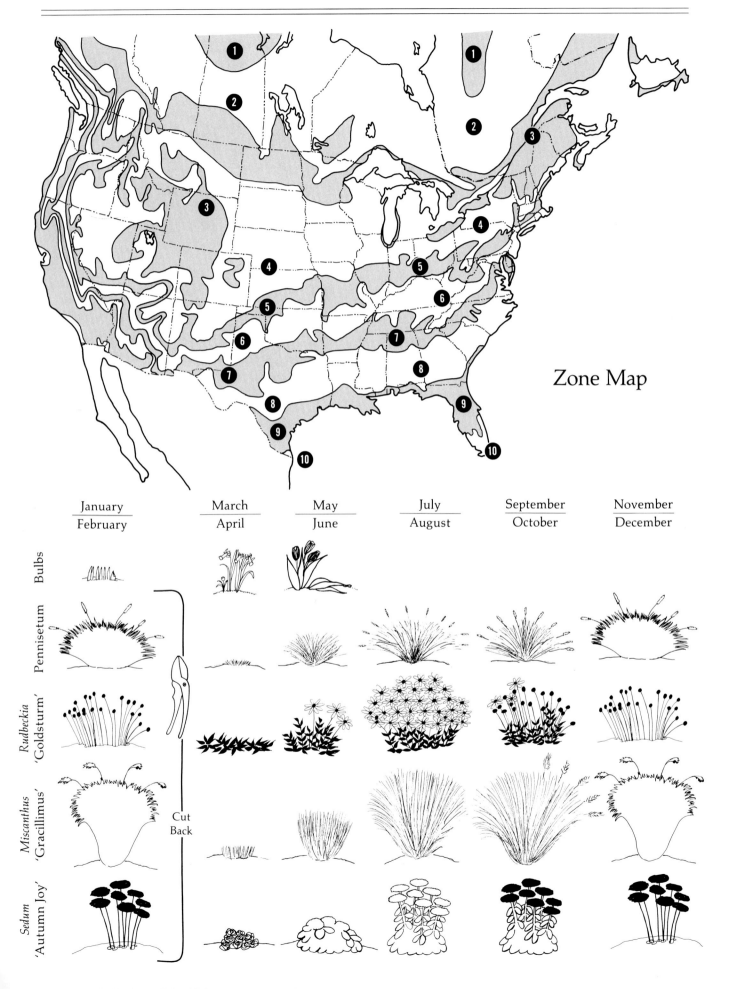

Zone Map

| January February | March April | May June | July August | September October | November December |

Forms of miscanthus: From lower left, clockwise, are medium-sized *M. purpurescens* which turns bright orange-red in fall; thick, lush Eulalia grass *(M. sinensis)*; giant miscanthus *(M. floridulus)*, which grows to nine feet; and yellow-banded porcupine grass *(M. sinensis zebrinus strictus)*.

until October, Korean reed grass is a low, bushy background plant that covers the ground neatly but without distinction. In October, however, the two-foot mound of gracefully arching foliage blooms in beautiful, white, foxtail-shaped flowers that shimmer in the sunlight. After frost the plant turns buff-colored, holding its flowers into winter. Once the plant declines in appearance, it should be cut back.

Deschampsia caespitosa 'Goldschleier' (Tufted Hair Grass): 'Goldschleier' tufted hair grass, hardy to zone 5, is a dense evergreen clump about two feet tall that develops the most delicate flowers of all the grasses in early summer. In mid-June to early July striking, large, lacy panicles are held erectly above the plants. Sturdy stems persist into winter. Tufted hair grass is also attractive in earliest spring with shiny, deep green spikes of leaves. A native of boggy soils the world over, tufted hair grass is effective all year and enjoys moist to average garden soil and sun or high shade. Propagate by division.

Molinia caerulea altissima 'Windspiel' (Tall Purple Moor Grass): 'Windspiel,' tall purple moor grass, is striking among the molinias for its outrageously long flower stalks that appear in July and remain on the plants well into winter. The height of stalks is variable, dependent upon site conditions. 'Windspiel' is an excellent specimen, especially when planted among massed perennials such as 'Autumn Joy' or evergreen ground covers like the prostrate junipers. The straight species, *Molinia caerulea,* is an adaptable grass whose flowering is variable, often at about five feet. Hardy to zone 5, it tolerates most garden situations, though it prefers moisture and an acid soil in full sun to light shade.

Miscanthus purpurescens (Purpurescens Silver Grass): Purpurescens silver grass looks like a miniature giant miscanthus in summer when it is a small, rather upright, three- to four-foot clump of broad, dark green blades. In fall, however, the entire plant turns a brilliant red-orange

Medium-sized grasses for sun: From top left, clockwise, are dramatic *Molinia caerulea altissima* 'Windspiel'; switch grass (*Panicum virgatum*), the best choice for outstanding winter presence; feather reed grass (*Calamagrostis x acutiflora stricta*), with erect flowers and seed heads; and fountain grass (*Pennisetum alopecuroides*).

which contrasts with the silvery white plumes that appear in August. After frost the brilliant fall coloration fades but still contrasts with lighter-colored winter grasses. Hardy to zone 5–6, this grass thrives in full sun. Propagate by division.

Panicum virgatum (Switch Grass): An American prairie native, hardy to zone 5, switch grass is an apple green, medium-sized grass that works well in masses, forming clouds of flower heads in August and drying into golden wheat-colored winter ground cover. The best for winter massing, switch grass tolerates a wide variety of soils and situations. It is effective from June until February when it is cut back. *Panicum virgatum* 'Rotstrahlbusch' is a smaller, red form of switch grass.

Pennisetum alopecuroides (Fountain Grass): Fountain grass, hardy to zone 5–6, forms a dense cushion of cascading foliage that is especially effective when used in masses in a sunny area. With companions like 'Au-

Grasses that tolerate shade: Clockwise from lower right are *Carex morowii variegata,* Japanese *Hakonechloa macra,* the dramatic drooping sedge (*Carex pendula*), *Spodiopogon sibiricus,* and delicate palm sedge (*Carex muskingumensis*).

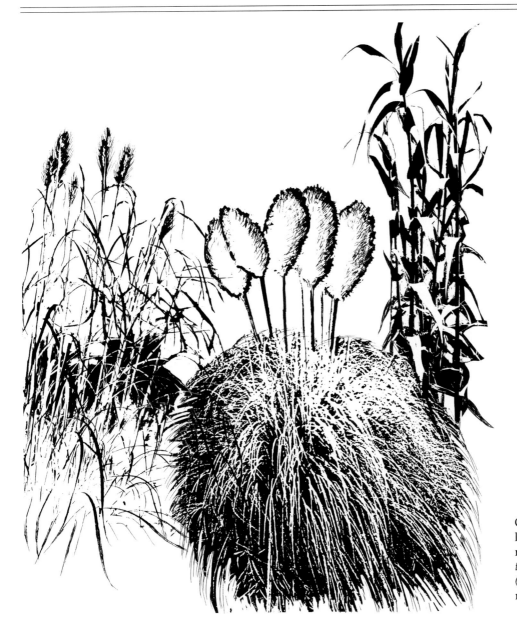

Grasses with presence: Sun-loving giants are, from left to right, Ravenna grass (*Erianthus ravennae*), pampas grass (*Cortaderia selloana*), and giant reed (*Arundo donax*).

tumn Joy' sedums or 'Goldsturm' rudbeckias, fountain grass combines in stunning stylized meadows. It blooms in July, with pinkish flower heads that blanch and remain on the plants into December. Fountain grass is effective from June until February, although it is more susceptible to wind damage and thus not as handsome as switch grass. Useful for gardeners in warm climates are other, more tender varieties of pennisetum: *P. alopecuroides f. viridescens* (zone 7) with black seed heads, *P. setaceum* (zone 8) with pink seed heads, and *P. orientale* (zone 7) with an exceptionally long period of bloom, from June until October. *Pennisetum alopecuroides* 'Hameln' is a smaller form of the species, growing to only

Phalaris arundinacea picta (Gardener's Garters): Gardener's garters, hardy to zone 4, grows fastest where conditions are best—on fertile, moist watersides and in ditches. Its rambunctious growth can be contained by less than ideal conditions. It is a good plant for a bad place. Growth is slow and steady, for example, in clay soils with less than full sun. Its bright green-and-white, two- to three-foot foliage is excellent at stabilizing soils and is attractive nearly all year. When its foliage looks unkempt, gardener's garters can be mowed down to swiftly renew itself. Propagate by division.

Spartina pectinata aureo-marginata (Prairie Cord Grass): Prairie cord grass, hardy to zone 5, is a wonderfully adaptable bright apple green American native with yellow marginal stripes. It tolerates sun, light shade, moist, or dry conditions. A coarse, leathery plant that grows to four feet, it is ideal for beach house plantings. Given good soil, it will spread quickly but can be easily controlled. In fall, prairie cord grass turns bright

Evergreen grasses: Counterclockwise from bottom left are *Carex morowii variegata,* brilliant green *Festuca scoparia,* tufted hair grass *(Deschampsia caespitosa),* blue oat grass *(Helictotrichon sempervirens),* and drooping sedge *(Carex pendula).*

Grasses with unusual flowers and seeds: From left to right are shade-tolerant northern sea oats *(Chasmanthium latifolium)*, Korean calamagrostis *(C. arundinacea brachytricha)* with white "foxtails" in fall, and drooping sedge *(Carex pendula)*.

yellow and later darkens to buff. It is effective from June into winter but is sometimes knocked down in heavy snows. Propagate by division.

Spodiopogon sibiricus: Spodiopogon is a medium-sized, four- to five-foot grass whose blades are held at right angles on erect, upright stalks. Rosy and delicate flowers appear in July and August. Grown in light shade and in an average garden condition, spodiopogon is hardy to zone 5, growing tallest in fertile humus. It has a neat appearance throughout the growing season. Effective from June until November, after frost spodiopogon turns brown. It is excellent used as a small specimen or in small groups.

Small-sized

Carex buchananii (Leatherleaf Sedge): A New Zealand native, the leatherleaf sedge, hardy to zone 6–7, is unusual both in leaf (narrow, curling cylinders that further curl at the tips) and color (a cinnamon bronze) all year. Best in groups in moist sun where the narrow, upright, two-foot habit and color are more effective. Nondescript flowers appear in June. Propagate by seed or division.

Carex morrowii variegata (Japanese Sedge): Japanese sedge forms an attractive and weed-proof evergreen mound with fine white margins on the leaves. Grown in shade and moderately moist soil or pots, Japanese sedge grows one foot tall. Inconspicuous flowers are formed in March. Although it is evergreen, it begins to look a bit weather-beaten in February and March, improving in mid-spring.

Carex muskingumensis (Palm Sedge): Palm sedge, a North American native hardy to zone 5, takes two years to fully develop in the garden.

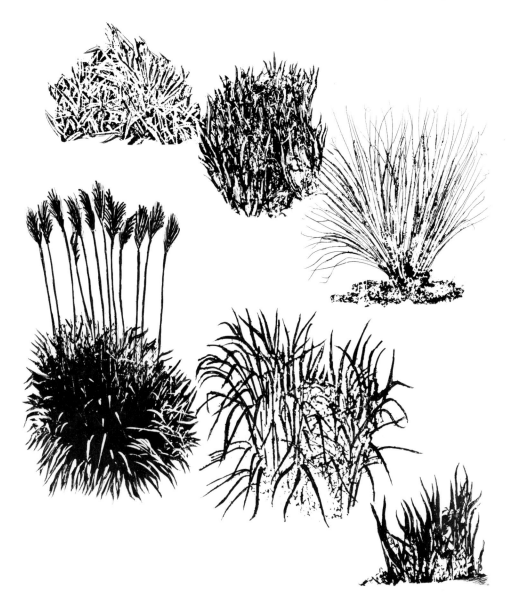

Grasses with unusual coloring: Top row, from left to right, are green-and-white gardener's garters *(Phalaris arundinacea picta),* Japanese blood grass *(Imperata cylinrica rubra* 'Red Baron'), and cinnamon-colored *Carex buchananii.* Bottom row shows, from left to right, *Miscanthus purpurescens,* modestly green all summer until it turns brilliant red-orange in fall; bright green prairie cord grass *(Spartina pectinata aureo-marginata),* which turns a bright clear yellow in fall; and blue lyme grass *(Elymus arenarius).*

Its primary use is in shady areas, where bright green leaves provide lush summer foliage. Frost turns palm sedge to shades of pale apricot and wheat that are attractive for a very short time. Growing in light to full shade, palm sedge is effective from June until winter. Propagate by seed or division.

Chasmanthium latifolium (Uniola) (Northern Sea Oats): Northern sea oats, so-called for the extremely showy drooping seed clusters on upright, broad, light green–leafed plants, is an American native hardy to zone 5. Its seeds turn white in September. Northern sea oats grow to four feet in full sun to part shade and prefer moist, cool soil. They flower in August.

Elymus arenarius (European Dune Grass or Lyme Grass): European dune grass, hardy to zone 4, grows to two feet of deep, glaucous blue. European dune grass, or lyme grass as it is sometimes called, blooms in late June and July on tall yellow stalks. It is rhizomatous, spreading easily and lending itself to beach plantings and other situations where a soil binder is practical. In ordinary garden soil, lyme grass needs re-straining. Propagate by seed or division.

Festuca: There are many fescues available for garden use. Most are glaucous blue-green, but a number are deep green. All are effective year-round and do best in full sun in soils of low fertility. They are hardy to zone 4–5. The following are some of the best of the many excellent fescues in cultivation: *Festuca cinerea* 'Klose,' a dark green, eight-inch mound; *Festuca cinerea* 'Solling,' a six-inch mound of powder blue-green; *Festuca scoparia* 'Pic carlit,' a very stiff, prickly mound of brilliant green; *Festuca muelleri,* growing to an eight-inch soft, blue-green mound; and *Festuca tenuifolia,* an eight-inch mound of fine, velvety, yellow-green foliage with deep, reddish bronze seed heads in spring and early summer.

Hakonechloa macra 'Aureola': Hakonechloa, hardy to zone 5, is a bright yellow-and-green variegated grass from Japan that is suitable for the shade garden. Arching up to eighteen inches from a narrow base, it may be used either as a specimen or in a mass planting. In masses it has the effect of sunlight falling on the plants.

Helictotrichon sempervirens (Blue Oat Grass): Blue oat grass forms a stiff, spiny cushion of twenty inches. Fine, clean, evergreen blue-gray foliage blooms in June on great arching panicles of blue-brown. These are extremely showy, held high above the plant. Not unlike a large fescue, blue oat grass, hardy to zone 5, remains low but will spread with age to as much as three feet. Propagate by seed or division.

Imperata cylindrica rubra 'Red Baron' (Japanese Blood Grass): Japanese blood grass, hardy to zone 5, is a small, upright, boldly colored grass from Japan, with a slow rhizomatous habit. It is stunning in combination with evergreens, prefers half to full shade, and grows to about eighteen inches tall. After frost, Japanese blood grass loses its brilliant color and becomes nondescript.

The Right Stuff

PLANTS, LIKE PEOPLE, come in endless variety. Most are pretty fair individuals who have their good points. A very few are outstanding—head and shoulders above the rest. They seem to have only positive attributes and do everything right. These are the plants with the right stuff, the ones to grow in the new garden.

In fact, selecting the right varieties for the new garden is a little like hiring extraordinary individuals for a demanding job. Not just anybody has the correct set of attributes to do the work satisfactorily. Although good looks are important, a pretty face isn't enough to get the job done. Plants for the new garden have to be self-starters and independent workers. They have to present themselves well, get along with others, and be reliable. They have to start early and stay late. Most important of all, they have to be happy in their situations. Only unusually talented individuals will answer the job description.

"Hiring" the right plants is further complicated by each garden's special requirements. Obviously, the job description for a garden in Oregon will be different from one in Arizona. No matter how much talent a plant has, it will not succeed in a Wisconsin garden if it doesn't tolerate ten below zero. If it needs regular rainfall, it will die in the southern California summer unless watered regularly. But rather than bemoan the characteristics of a given site or climate, American gardeners must learn to capitalize on the unique attributes of their gardens and their regions.

Sturdy and beautiful, plants with the right stuff are carefully placed but allowed to grow without constant intervention. Here, velvety red daylilies and golden 'Goldsturm' rudbeckias contrast with a feather reed grass (*Calamagrostis x acutiflora stricta*).

From the group of plants suited to each region, only the best of the best are chosen to work in the new American garden. Once its suitability has been ascertained, a plant's next most important characteristics are the length, quality, and reliability of its performance. The plant has to look good, contributing to the overall appearance of the garden, for the longest possible time. It has to work well in sequence with other plants. Bloom is important, but not to the exclusion of foliage.

Good, clean, attractive foliage that doesn't need outside assistance—staking, tying, or spraying—is a prerequisite for a plant's inclusion in the new garden. Also necessary is a long period of bloom. Deadheading—removing the spent flowers from plants after bloom—is too labor-intensive; flowers that turn into attractive seed heads provide a second, subdued period of "bloom." Leaving seed heads on the plants lengthens the period of show while saving labor.

In temperate regions, winter appearance is all-important. A few herbaceous plants present themselves well in winter, most notably grasses like miscanthus, pennisetum, and panicum. Juxtaposing such plants with evergreen material makes for striking winter interest.

In order to work well in the new garden, a plant has to be the kind of individual that can be counted upon, with desirable qualities such as the length and profusion of bloom, longevity, neat habit, and lustrous, attractive foliage. Plant breeders seek to develop such individuals. Hybrids that exhibit improvements over the straight species are constantly being developed. The best place to see these hybrids and how they perform is in a garden; many arboreta have demonstration gardens with displays designed to educate the home gardener. High-quality plants can also be seen in high-quality nurseries.

The plants listed in this chapter are, for the most part, generalists. They require regular rainfall and, in most instances, a temperate climate. Gardeners from high altitudes or arid or semi-tropical climates will have to call in specialists. Botanical gardens and local nurseries that specialize in native and climate-appropriate plants can provide information. Gardeners should also be inventive and look not only in catalogs and nursery centers but in their own backyards for interesting and well-adapted "weeds."

The following list of plants with the right stuff has been selected for its versatility; however, not all plants will be suitable in all geographic areas of the United States. Information about hardiness zones and microclimates has been included.

Achillea filipendulina (Fernleaf Yarrow): Yarrows provide excellent long-lived high ground cover in the new garden. They are hardy everywhere in the United States, requiring only full sun, good drainage, and an open position. In July, yarrows bloom in flat flower clusters on tall, very erect stalks. Seed heads may be left on the plants throughout the winter, when their soft taupes contrast with the dusty green of evergreen foliage. Although *A. f.* 'Golden Plate' is the largest and most spectacular

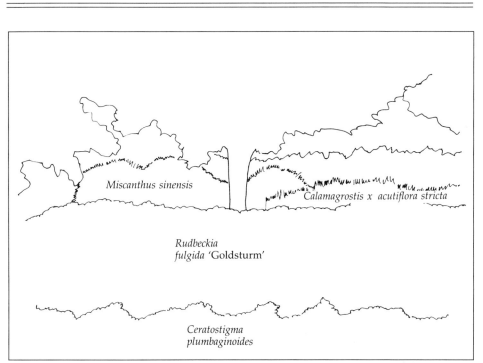

Miscanthus sinensis

Calamagrostis x acutiflora stricta

*Rudbeckia
fulgida* 'Goldsturm'

*Ceratostigma
plumbaginoides*

Lookalikes for the native black-eyed Susan, masses of an outstanding variety of *Rudbeckia fulgida* 'Goldsturm' bloom prolifically from July until September on uniform two-foot plants. Here, a berm of 'Goldsturm' rudbeckias is edged by blue-blooming leadwort (*Ceratostigma plumbaginoides*). Visible behind the 'Goldsturm' rudbeckias are the seed heads of feather reed grass (*Calamagrostis x acutiflora stricta*) and graceful mounds of maiden grass (*Miscanthus sinensis* 'Gracillimus').

A broad sweep of sun-loving achilleas is an excellent and long-lasting landscape feature. After blooms fade, stiff, taupe-colored seed heads may be left on the plants for winter texture. Easy to start from seed, achilleas bloom in their second year.

yarrow, blooming in flat, six-inch flower clusters on five-foot stems, the three-foot-high *A. f.* 'Coronation Gold' is a better choice in the new garden because it requires no staking unless it is overfed. Yarrows tolerate drought and poor soil. A block of 'Coronation Gold' serves as dramatic ground cover that blends well with a yellow-striped grass such as porcupine grass, *Miscanthus sinensis zebrinus strictus,* and lemon yellow–flowered threadleaf coreopsis.

Alchemilla mollis (Lady's Mantle): Lady's mantle is a low, spreading ground cover, hardy to zone 3 and suitable in most soils and partial shade. While it prefers a well-drained but moist soil, it will grow even in the dry shade of large trees. For two months lady's mantle blooms in yellow-green stalks of flowers that are held up over mounding plants. In bloom, lady's mantle has a wonderful lushness that is hard to achieve in a less-than-ideal garden spot.

Armeria maritima (Common Thrift): With good drainage and sun, thrift will grow virtually anywhere in the country. It is hardy to zone 3, preferring dry, infertile soil and tolerating wind, salt spray, and a sandy soil. It grows from evergreen, grasslike clumps of foliage about five inches tall and is very easy to start from seed. Globose flowers in pinks, fuchsias, and white bloom in June and July and sporadically afterwards. They are held high above the plants on erect stems from six to twelve inches tall. The variety 'Bees Ruby' is larger, sending up eighteen-inch stems of pink flowers. Armerias are neat, long-lived, and forgiving of neglect. Thrift is useful in small places, as a finishing plant around larger perennials, or all by itself as lawn.

Astilbe arendsii (Hybrid Astilbe): Given moist, rich soil and good drainage, especially in winter, astilbes will thrive in sun or light shade, providing excellent ferny foliage, a long, striking period of bloom beginning in June, and attractive seed heads that can be left on the plants for winter interest. Astilbes are hardy and grow from zones 4 through 8. Their large plumelike blooms come in white, pink, and red. 'Red Sentinel' and white 'Bridal Veil' are excellent cultivars. Excellent massed in the landscape is the tall *A. tacquetii superba,* which grows to four feet and blooms in deep rose. Astilbes are good plants to follow daffodils or tulips because their red, lacy emerging leaves are an attractive foil to the sprawling after-bloom foliage of bulbs.

Bergenia: Bergenias will grow almost anywhere, from zones 4 through 10, except Florida, tolerating dry or moist spots, various soils, sun or shade. Their bold leathery leaves are evergreen and blush with exposure to sun, turning bronze after frost. In the new garden, large masses of bergenias are more valued for their multicolored leaf texture in winter than for the flower clusters that appear above the plants in spring.

Ceratostigma plumbaginoides (Leadwort): Leadwort is a spreading, blue-flowering, low ground cover that is hardy and grows in zones 6 to 10 with good drainage. Planted in sun or light shade, ten-inch plants will bloom for a month or more beginning in July. After the blue flowers

Feathery switch grass *(Panicum virgatum)* is the longest lasting medium-sized grass, keeping its form throughout winter despite wind and storm. Glowing golden on a rainy December morning, it lights up the spaces under River birch *(Betula nigra)* in a small Washington park.

There is a daylily (hemerocallis) for every garden. Attractive, shade-tolerant, drought-tolerant, and free from insect pests, a clump of daylilies can be counted upon to perform in any garden. New varieties exhibiting colors ranging from red, shown here, to salmon, pale yellow, and gold are available. A recent introduction, golden yellow, prize-winning 'Stella d'Oro,' blooms longer than any other daylily. It starts in May and repeat blooms every three weeks or so into fall.

fade, attractive red flower bracts add interest in the fall. Later, upper leaves turn reddish, adding attractively colored texture to the fall garden. Planting leadwort is an excellent way of covering the ground around and between taller, leggier ground covers.

Calamagrostis x acutiflora stricta (Reed Grass): 'Karl Foerster' feather reed grass is a sturdy, robust-growing, and extremely showy five-foot grass that blooms in June. Fluffy, pink-tinged flowers stiffen into striking wheat-colored seed heads held erect above very upright plants from late June until winter. Reliably hardy to zone 5, 'Karl Foerster' will survive farther north where there is a snow cover. Its distinctly upright habit makes it remarkable as a small specimen or in accent groups of three or more arising from lower ground cover.

Coreopsis verticillata (Threadleaf Coreopsis): The thread-leaved coreopsis grows in full sun and poor soil from zones 4 through 10. Blooming all summer, with golden and yellow daisylike flowers on fine, soft, two-foot mounds of medium green foliage, it tolerates drought and neglect and is long-lived. After frost, the foliage turns bright green with dark seed heads for a while before darkening to gray-brown clouds in winter. 'Moonbeam' is a two-foot lemon yellow–colored cultivar. *C. v. grandiflora* is a golden yellow that grows to three feet.

Epimedium: Epimediums grow almost anywhere in zones 3 to 8 that is moist enough, but they prefer light shade. In spring their heart-shaped leaves are bright yellow-green, carried on delicate stems. In May small rose, lavender, yellow, or white flowers are held on long stems above the twelve-inch plants. Yellow epimedium *(E. sulphureum)* spreads the fastest and is larger than the choice, slow-growing *E. niveum*, which blooms white. Epimediums serve as excellent camouflage for the disheveled foliage of bulbs after bloom. They develop fresh, new leaves as late daffodils bloom.

Hemerocallis (Daylily): Daylilies grow virtually anywhere in the country from zone 3 down to the Gulf Coast. The farther south they are grown, the more shade they require and vice versa. In average soil and good drainage a clump of daylilies will expand slowly but steadily, faring well with root competition from trees and shrubs. Because daylilies are grouped into early, mid-, and late-season plants, the gardener can plan for sequential bloom or have daylilies' flowering dovetail with that of other perennials. Their clumps of straplike foliage emerge after bulbs bloom, serving as good camouflage. Small varieties grow about twenty inches tall while large ones reach three feet and more. Flowers tend to bloom toward the sun, a trait to be kept in mind when placing them. Virtually thousands of varieties are available in yellows, oranges, salmon, pink, red, and mahogany. 'Hyperion,' an old favorite, is still a good yellow.

Hosta: Hostas, hardy to zone 3, are shade-loving plants grown for their foliage. Except in soggy soil, hostas are virtually indestructible, growing slowly but steadily even in the dry shade of large trees. In decent soil their performance is outstanding. Many variegated hostas have been developed. When used in large masses in shade, variegation has the look of sunlight-struck foliage. To bring light to a dark part of the garden choose *H. fortunei picta,* which has yellow leaves until June when it blooms and its leaves turn green. Hosta leaves open when late tulips bloom.

Liriope: Liriope is a deep green wonder plant—indestructible and tolerant of sun or shade. Although it prefers moisture, it withstands drought. Big blue liriope *(L. muscari)* grows in zone 6 and southward. The creeping liriope *(L. spicata)* is hardier, thriving in zone 4. Both bloom in August, with lavender flower clusters that look a little like grape hyacinths. Black berries follow the flowers. From zone 6, liriopes are evergreen, although by February their leaves are weather-beaten. Cutting back the old leaves in spring keeps the plants neat. Liriopes are excellent cover for daffodils.

Miscanthus sinensis 'Silberfeder' (Silverfeather Grass): Silverfeather grass, very similar to maiden grass but blooming reliably in colder climates, grows to a dense, graceful, six-foot mound of elegantly pendant foliage. It is the first of the large miscanthus grasses to bloom, sending up showy, silvery white plumes in August. These are held on the plant throughout the winter, and the plant turns almond color after frost. Rated as hardy zone 5, silverfeather grass is reported to grow in more northerly regions where there is a snow cover.

Pennisetum alopecuroides (Fountain Grass): Fountain grass, reliable and handsome from June until February, when its almond-colored winter foliage is cut back, is a carefree garden treasure. Bright new green blades emerge as tulips bloom, masking dying foliage later. By June fountain grass forms a lush, full clump that cascades as the season progresses. Showy seed heads, which are effective through September, form in July. After frost, particularly when planted in masses, fountain grass has the luminous winter presence of a field of glowing wheat. It should be cut back in mid to late February before new growth begins. Hardy to zone 5–6, fountain grass grows to a three- or four-foot-high cascading mound that can reach four feet across after three years in full sun.

Rudbeckia fulgida 'Goldsturm' (Black-eyed Susans): 'Goldsturm' rudbeckias are one of the longest flowering, most carefree plants anywhere. 'Goldsturm' rudbeckias begin flowering in July, completely covering stocky, dark green, two-foot plants that are attractive and present through most of the year. They continue to bloom into September, after which attractive chocolate brown seed pods are formed in great number. These are held on the plants through winter—an interesting, attractive feature that is especially effective when plants are massed. Thriving in sun or light shade in zones 3 to 10, these rudbeckias are a far cry from the native black-eyed Susan lookalikes. 'Goldsturm' is an excellent choice for a stylized meadow planting.

Sedum telephium 'Autumn Joy': It has been called "one of the best plants

A plant for all seasons and all places, *Sedum telephium* 'Autumn Joy' starts out the year quietly pale green and pink but later turns brilliant copper red. It performs in virtually all garden situations including high shade. In winter, stiff seed heads may be seen poking through the snow.

An early blooming and very beautiful variety of miscanthus, *M. sinensis* 'Silberfeder' is in full flower by mid-September. Its colorful companion is another miscanthus, porcupine grass (*M. sinensis zebrinus strictus*).

ever developed." Wonderful adaptable, it thrives from zones 3 through 10 in virtually any soil, in full sun or light shade. 'Autumn Joy' reaches twenty inches of succulent pale green foliage that is neat from the time it begins active growth in April until frost. Its large, flat flower umbels begin as green plates and turn to a soft rose color in late August, darkening to a rich copper red. After frost the flower umbels darken to coppery brown and are held on the plants throughout the winter.

Stachys byzantina (Lamb's Ears): Lamb's ears thrive from zones 3 through 10—virtually anywhere in the country except Florida and around the Gulf Coast. It is a trouble-free, twelve-inch mound of fuzzy, silvery green foliage that prefers full sun and very well-drained soil. Spreading steadily, lamb's ears may be divided in spring or fall. Tall flower stalks appear in June on most varieties. S. 'Silver Carpet' is one that does not flower. The plant's low, silvery foliage is an excellent, easy-care ground cover that is especially effective around an outdoor living area at night. It is also handsome near bulbs in early spring because it is attractive before other perennials have made much growth.

*Room
with a View*

SPACE IN THE NEW GARDEN is divided into two areas:
one planted in magnificent, dynamic ground cover and the other with
no-nonsense, functional paving. A paved space, accessible to the inside
of the house, hidden from the street and neighbors, is the heart of the
garden. This is where the gardener views his realm, where the outdoor
living, reading, relaxing, sun-soaking, and entertaining is done. The
paved space also functions as a clearing through which the garden is
viewed from inside the house.

Paving is for people. It is security underfoot when the terrain is wet,
uneven, or obstructed. It is a projection of the man-made into the natural, defining the limits of both. Like a boat on water, paving is a means
of venturing from one realm to another in safety and comfort.

Because by its nature paving will clearly define planted and living
areas, the space around it can be wild and full—unruly nature at its
spontaneous best. When the contrast between the smooth, comfortable
surface underfoot and opulent vegetation is great, the garden has it all:
a safe, dry, creature-comfortable island in the middle of exciting, exuberant nature. It has lights and chairs and the Sunday paper amid the
sound of birds and crickets and a jungle of lush herbaceous vegetation.

As the natural landscape around American cities succumbs to development, the longing for green, untrammeled nature escalates. As clogged
streets, parking lots, shopping centers, and other people's backyards

Moving through a jungle of
plants, a paved path leads to
an outdoor living area that is
enclosed and nearly hidden in
an exuberant planting of ornamental grasses and perennials. Joe Pye weed
(*Eupatorium purpureum*) mingles with evergreens, grasses,
and red blooming hibiscus.

blight the horizon, one's own small backyard becomes the single constant vision of soul-renewing nature. Planted as a rectangle of lawn, such a vision will slowly starve the soul. Planned and planted to respond to the seasons, brimming with opulent planting, an ordinary backyard can become a spa for the spirit.

The first consideration for turning a yard into an outdoor room is a view. In a handful of cases an outdoor space is blessed with a vista: the sea, a woodland, mountains on the horizon. In these instances the garden is opened up to the view by channeling vision toward the natural splendor. Trees and large grasses, low walls and rows of potted plants may frame the view, while rivers of ground cover move toward it. Paving, benches, tables, and chairs are oriented toward it. In this situation plants, paving, and other garden elements augment what is already there.

Most often, however, there is no existing view. Neighboring houses may tower over the garden, or an alley may run behind it. In this case the garden itself provides or, indeed, becomes the view. In some gardens paving may be oriented in one direction and a vista constructed by layering plants and, possibly, installing a focus. A gazebo, a sculptural plant, sculpture, a striking tree—all serve both to draw and stop the eye.

In other situations, furnishings—a table and chairs, a chaise longue and table, even a single chair—call attention to themselves and suggest the sense of a comfortable place. Little else is needed. Pots of flowering annuals grouped around furniture add a splash of color. Areas surrounding such a terrace are densely planted for privacy.

Pools, whether for fish or for people, rivet attention. A pool is to a garden what a fireplace is to a room. It is a gathering place, a source of comfort, a focus. In summer, the mere appearance of water seems to lower temperature.

Fish pools are of relatively low maintenance in comparison to the enjoyment, interest, and good looks they add. Placed immediately adjacent to a terrace, the pool with its fish, water plants, and the inevitable toads and birds who come uninvited will enliven the garden. Attention will be centered on the pool and the living area. The garden beyond may be planted in lush layers for privacy. An added plus is water gardening, a delightful garden subspecialty with its own plant palette. Sun-loving water lilies are available in both tropical and hardy types. Cattails and floating aquatic species enlarge the offerings.

Sculpture also belongs in the outdoor room. Like the paving underfoot, it extends the man-made into nature in a juxtaposition of unlikes that is often dramatic but sometimes whimsical. Large pieces serve as powerful foci; smaller ones become weatherproof reference points. Sculpture needn't be art. Rocks, small trees, large perennials, birdhouses, gateways, gazebos, groups of potted plants may be three-dimensional elements that command attention and belong in a transitional space. All of these elements serve well in the ever-changing seasonal displays of herbaceous plantings.

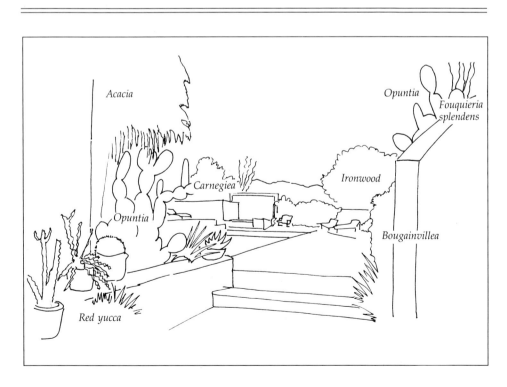

Elements of this Arizona garden's outdoor room enhance splendid scenery. Pool and paving channel vision toward it, while a sheltering wall and trees frame the mountain view. Arid climate plants, used throughout the garden, are in keeping with the landscape around it.
(Photo and design by Steve Martino & Associates)

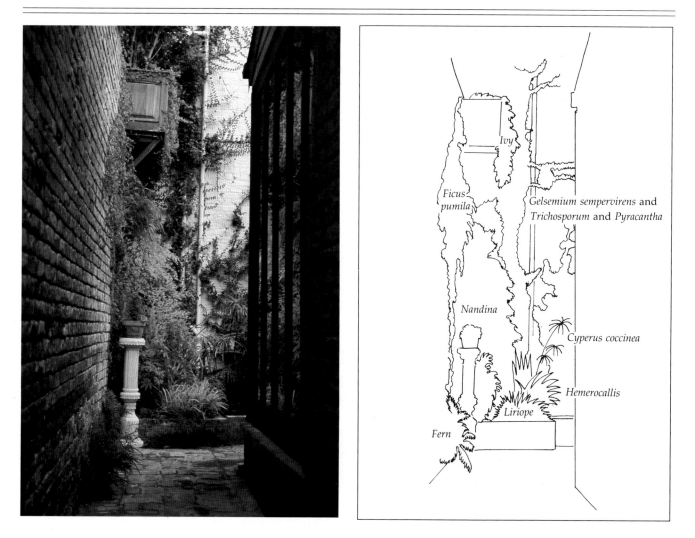

A small pool serves as the focus of a narrow passageway leading to Al and Zide Hirt's small garden in New Orleans's French Quarter. Because of the garden's diminutive size, brick paving covers most of the ground. Sturdy plants—ivy, creeping fig, nandina, liriope, pyracantha—in containers on the ground and suspended from the walls soften the hard brick surface.

(Design by Christopher Fischer)

Plants with great presence—mammoth grasses and perennials—are living sculpture. The giant ornamental grasses, *Miscanthus floridulus, Erianthus ravennae,* and moisture-loving *Arundo donax,* provide not only dynamic form but movement and sound. Small trees with multistems and interesting bark make excellent three-dimensional sculptures that do not overpower or drastically alter light. The birches—canoe birch *(Betula papyrifera)* for the North and River birch *(Betula nigra)* for the South—crape myrtle (lagerstroemia), lace bark pine *(Pinus bungeana),* and showy stewartia *(Stewartia ovata grandiflora)* are only a few good small trees. A large herbaceous perennial like plume poppy *(Macleaya cordata),* heracleum, or rodgersia, with large shapely leaves, acts as a dramatic focus against masses of more homogeneous ground cover.

Space in even the tiniest garden may be manipulated to make it seem larger. Paved areas should be made large and not necessarily run at right angles to the lot lines. The lawn, in all but the largest yards, should be eliminated, since it not only complicates maintenance chores but minimizes apparent space.

Fences yield the most privacy for the least amount of space. When

Sculpture serves as an all-season focus, enhancing or creating a view. Here, a stone cherub provides the finishing touch to the border of a gravel terrace.

planted with vines like ivy or rapidly growing silver lace vine (poly-gonum) or espaliered with shrubs like euonymus, fences add a sense of great green depth to even a shallow yard. Steps, gates, or paths leading into even the tiniest garden greatly enhance apparent space. Likewise, large open plants in the foreground create depth.

Masses of magnificent ground cover of different heights and flower-ing times enrich the viewer's experience while enlarging the garden log-ically. In a long, narrow space these masses might be arranged in layers to suggest unending space. Ornamental grasses of enormous volume, *Miscanthus sinensis* 'Gracillimus' or the variegated *Miscanthus sinensis zebrinus strictus*, flanking a sitting area create a wonderfully secluded, sheltered space. Their volumes, too, suggest great depth.

Using masses of perennials of different heights combines unity with variety. Each single mass is weighty enough to hold its own in the land-scape, yet shares the limelight with other masses that bloom and draw attention at different times. The combination is rich without becoming spotty. Different heights create layers, suggesting great depth and lend-ing the garden a wild, loose, flowing air.

Very tall plants, such as *Arundo donax, Miscanthus floridulus,* or *Ma-cleaya cordata*, punctuate the layers of massed ground cover to direct view, neutralize colors, screen, and provide a space-enhancing fore-ground. In spring their rapid growth amazes as it changes the aspect of the garden in only a few quick weeks. As few other plants do, these giant perennials occupy the garden's volume where impact is most powerful: at and slightly above eye level.

Any paved place out of doors is a transitional space between inside and out. Its unique status dictates special materials. Because it will be lived in, it is furnished for comfortable use. Because it is open to wind and sun and rain, furnishings are simple, impervious to the elements. Treated wood, plastics, metal, canvas, and stone are at home outside. In their clean simplicity, these minimal furnishings allow for freedom from care while supplying some of the creature comforts of inside places.

Simply furnished, roomy paved spaces extend living areas outside. Flat green rectangles of backyards with little promise, hemmed in by alleys and buildings and cursed with a topsoil of builder's fill, can be transformed into mysterious repositories of luxuriant and spontaneous vegetation. When they are encircled by deep, lush layers of magnificent ground cover, the living experience is like no other. Such gardens re-fresh and rejuvenate the spirit. No longer the source of mindless main-tenance, the new garden becomes an urban oasis for plants, for wildlife, and, not least, for the world-weary.

Extending the living area out-doors, the paving of this Lou-isiana courtyard is contiguous with indoor space. Confined to containers, lush plants soften stone surfaces while ta-bles and chairs suggest a sense of place.
(Design by Christopher Friedrichs)

The New American Gardener

"LANDSCAPING IS not a complex and difficult art to be practiced only by high priests. It is logical, down-to-earth, and aimed at making your plot of ground produce exactly what you want and need from it." So wrote Thomas Church, a landscape architect whose residential designs in the forties and fifties addressed the ordinary problems and practical needs of people living in typical houses on small lots. In addition to wanting a soul-renewing garden and an outdoor space in which to enjoy it, Church realized, people have cars to be parked, trash to be stored for pickup, and garden paraphernalia to be kept available. His designs mixed together the sublime and the mundane in beautiful and functional ways.

Planning the space—allocating places for parking, service, beauty, and living—must be done first. The impulse to rush out and plant flowers and to run to the nursery for the best-looking trees and shrubs has to be quelled. Planning comes first. Without an overall plan, a gardener is likely to end up with plantings along existing paths or house walls in predictable rows—to organize his garden along lines set down arbitrarily by a developer or builder.

A plat plan, a drawing of a house and lot in scale with property lines shown, available from a county zoning office, is enormously helpful in laying out paths and patios where they are most needed and used. Although walking around the property to experience the views and mood of each area is essential, a plat plan is an aid in plotting the path of the

Maintenance chores can be simplified by grouping together plants with similar cultural needs. In this California garden, plants that require irrigation, such as the dazzling coreopsis blooming here, are grouped together in planters near the house. Farther from the house is a nonirrigated garden of succulents and cacti.

sun in summer and winter so that landscape elements such as large masses of ground cover, larger plants, paving, shade trees, and pergolas may be sited effectively. The gardener should do both: combine work with a plan for an understanding of the total space and walk around the property to determine the characteristics of each part. That way, he will also be able to identify its microclimates correctly.

From Germany comes a new system for growing and placing plants. Categorized by *Lebensbereich,* which means "life zone" or cultural niche, each plant is labeled by the place in which it occurs in nature. Typical categories include Woodland, Woodland's Edge, Field, and Moor. The idea is that plants from areas with the same climatic conditions—rainfall, sunlight, temperature—will thrive wherever conditions of the original habitat occur, even on different continents. Thus, plants from the deserts of the entire world would grow together more easily than plants from all the geographical areas of a single country.

In this system of classification, many cultivated perennials are classed as "Border," a niche whose plants require the highest degree of maintenance. In addition to high-strung cultivated perennials, other plants grouped in the Border niche are those growing under conditions dissimilar to those of their native habitat. This system recognizes that maintenance chores go up when plants venture out of the naturally occurring conditions that characterize their native habitats.

By correctly identifying the conditions that prevail in a garden site, the gardener will eliminate years of trial and error in the garden's development. One thing to be taken into consideration is that man requires plants to grow in conditions that do not exist in nature. For example, plants growing in the dank shade on the north side of a large building will not have the soil-drying root competition of a woodland. The best plants for the conditions may be those that originate in saturate soils. A northern garden sited in the teeth of the winter winds—especially where wind velocity has been enhanced by the channeling effect of buildings and streets—may need grasses and perennials from the tundra. It is up to the gardener to interpret the man-made microclimate.

In places where the natural landscape has been destroyed by development—which is almost everywhere—it is up to gardeners to reconstitute a natural landscape. Unfortunately, just letting the yard grow as it will is likely to be aesthetically unappealing. The goal of the new garden is to find the happy medium between the randomness of nature and the human penchant for satisfying order. Planting easy, flowing plants like grasses and excellent perennials in a seemingly random fashion is a way of ordering a natural look. Control is exerted before planting; after installation, the plants take care of themselves.

The better the fit of plants to the microclimate, the more successful the garden will be. If plants are healthy the garden will not only look natural and require less upkeep but will begin to behave like a naturally

Planning the space comes first in landscape architect Jack Chandler's own Napa Valley garden. Instead of being lined up at right angles to lot lines, garden elements, pool, terrace, and pergola, channel vision toward a vista of mountains on the horizon. Paving is softened by clumps of fountain grass.

A single path serves both entrance and maintenance needs. Large enough to channel circulation and be a pleasant place to be, it magnifies apparent space as it cuts down on planted area to be maintained. Here, a lush combination of arid climate natives flanks the entrance path and stairway to an Arizona house. Overhead, a Chilean mesquite casts cooling shade. Agaves punctuate a ground cover of *Acacia redolens* while bougainvillea adds a dash of color.
(Design by Steve Martino & Associates)

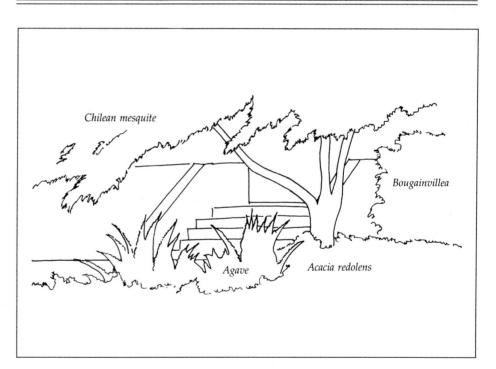

occurring community. Plants well suited to the cultural niche will be able to naturalize and take off on their own. The process that was interrupted by development can begin again in individual gardens.

After the unique conditions of site have been determined, planning next involves considerations of circulation and outdoor living needs. In today's gardens, utilitarian considerations must become beautiful elements of the garden's design. Cultural niches, paths, outdoor living space, and utility areas must come together in a beautiful, functional whole.

> *There is no reason for anyone to tiptoe around his garden as if it were a Ming dynasty vase. . . . Utility and beauty are not incompatible details.*
>
> —Thomas Church

In the days of vast estates—or even roomy yards—people thought first about vistas and allees and perennial borders; the nastier details— trash cans, car parks, service areas—simply ended up in the leftover space. Today's lots are often so small that these details must be addressed first, and creatively, to allow room for anything else. Nobody would think of putting in separate service and entrance driveways today, but a surprising number of people have duplicate paths leading around the house to the backyard.

> *Too many roads and walks are enemies to good landscape views as well as to economy.*
>
> —William Robinson

Too many half-developed paths and paved areas are distracting and detract from the yard's overall appearance. One generous, beautiful, comfortable path, planted for beauty and ease of upkeep, can serve both entrance and maintenance needs. Made bigger, it will not only do the job and be a pleasant place to be but will magnify apparent space even as it cuts down on the size of planted areas to be maintained. Ideally, the path leads from the street to a front entrance, where it swells to a comfortable gathering space. It then continues around the house to a private area, where it culminates in the largest possible paved area the yard will hold.

> *Do not be afraid of large paved surfaces on terraces and entrance courts . . . for the average house on a small lot the amount of paving can be greatly increased without robbing us of the fundamental pleasures of a garden. . . . Hard, uncompromising lines in the garden can be softened, to almost any extent desired, by planting. . . . A terrace provides a transitional stage between the house and garden as well as adding an outdoor room.*
>
> —Thomas Church

In fact, the contrast between the hard surface of paving or decking and the soft lushness of exuberant foliage is one of the greatest charms of a garden. Paving allows people to venture into the depths of garden, to be surrounded by verdure, to experience nature *and* keep their feet dry. It is the best of two worlds. Paved areas should be as large as possible, with the areas around them densely planted with layers of magnificent ground cover.

There is a tendency for people to be timid about paving and to cling to outmoded conventions. One often sees very small yards in which a cramped terrace and skimpy planting beds flank a central lawn; the lawn dominates everything, demanding constant busywork, pushing the other, more delightful and functional garden elements aside. In areas of the country with adequate rainfall to keep the grass growing and in need of periodic mowing, this type of landscaping may be passed off as simply bad or nondesign. In arid regions, the demands this landscaping makes in the face of a worsening water shortage are nothing short of wasteful.

"Hard, uncompromising lines," said Thomas Church, "can be softened to almost any extent desired, by planting." Here, voluptuous specimens of fountain grass *(Pennisetum alopecuroides),* 'Autumn Joy' sedums, and switch grass *(Panicum virgatum)* in seed blur the edges of a flagstone patio.

Today's typical yard—with its traditional, large lawn, its mandatory evergreens across the front of the house, and its few street trees—if shored up with a sit-on mower, electric trimmers, and bags of fertilizers and herbicides, or a maintenance service that brings in all that stuff, is one of the most unrewarding, resource-consuming, and expensive yards imaginable. . . . Gardeners of this traditional style are more apt to spend their time trying to figure out why the lawn has dead spots or what disease afflicts the roses than enjoying a bird's song or taking pleasure in the progress of the native wildflowers.

—Rosalind Creasy

Most people have no reason to plant lawn. It is done purely out of habit. Today's life-style is better served by eliminating it. Dividing the yard into only two elements—paved areas for circulation and outdoor living, and garden for beauty and refreshment—simplifies upkeep. Generous planting areas allow for greater privacy and more spectacular display. Generous paving or decking adds to the house an outdoor room of near manorial proportions that magnifies apparent space.

Paving for circulation or an outdoor living area is the framework supporting the rest of the garden—the "bones" that hold it together. It is in relation to this framework that plants are placed, that views are constructed or blocked.

A paved living space is also a transitional space, a bridge between inside and out, with man-made and natural furnishings. Sculpture, birds, tables and chairs, squirrels, giant grasses, dynamic perennials, all belong in this special place between two worlds. Surrounding the outdoor room is the garden area where one experiences nature, where the seasons are played out in the plants chosen, where tensions and traffic are forgotten, where the eye can take in what is restful, green, and growing.

Deep down inside the soul of animal-man is a longing for these things, a desire sometimes compelling, sometimes quiescent, but always there. . . . Many of contemporary man's ailments—his hypertensions and his neuroses—are clearly no more than the physical evidence of his rebellion against his physical environment and his frustration at the widening gap between the environment he yearns for and the stifling artificial one we planners have so far provided for him.

—John Ormsbee Simonds

More and more, backyards—even the tiniest ones—are becoming refuges, not only for their owners but for plants and wildlife. In today's overbuilt, overurbanized world, with swiftly diminishing open space, even the tiniest gardens bear a great burden in serving as a single and constant representation of the world of nature. The garden, a severely limited number of square feet, must embody all of Nature's delight, her seasonal rhythms, her beauty, fragrance, romance, and mystery. Because pristine, untrammeled nature exists only in remote areas, people no longer have easy access to it. Only by consciously reconstituting a natural landscape, by setting up conditions for a community of loose, flowing plants to naturalize and to behave spontaneously, will the long-

Horticulturist and landscape architect Wolfgang Oehme's collection of loose, flowing plants lends a natural, almost wild air to his garden. Layers of vegetation surround and protect this lovely and mysterious secret garden in a typical suburban backyard.

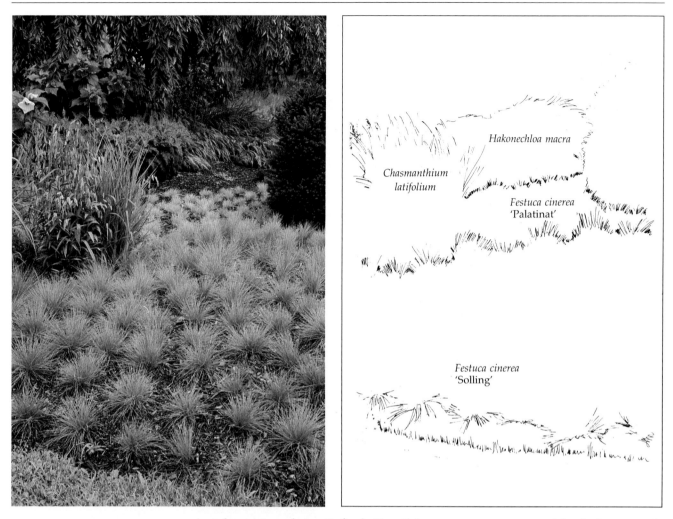

Hakonechloa macra

Chasmanthium latifolium

Festuca cinerea 'Palatinat'

Festuca cinerea 'Solling'

There is a grass to integrate into virtually any landscape. Here, a field of bright blue fescues (*Festuca cinerea* 'Solling') in foreground, backed by *Festuca cinerea* 'Palatinat,' leads back to a shade-loving, all-green form of hakonechloa, H. macra. At right is shade-tolerant northern sea oats (*Chasmanthium latifolium*). *(Photo by Monika Burwell)*

ing for nature be satisfied. For this reason, grasses, with their natural, almost wild-looking forms, make excellent subjects for the new garden. When massed they suggest prairie, meadow, or, to some, the savannah.

> . . . *these grasses are often massed. I would not be surprised to see a lion peer out.*
>
> —Henry Mitchell

In nature, grasses are a part of every landscape. Not only is there a grass that visually integrates into virtually any landscape, there is also a biologically suitable grass for every situation. Grasses' graceful, flowing habits conform to today's easy, natural style. Their rapid growth, low-maintenance requirements, late bloom, and outstanding winter appearance make them valuable garden subjects. In spite of a wild, spontaneous look, their growth is predictable. Even "giant" grasses like *Miscanthus sinensis* 'Gracillimus' won't outgrow their spaces or alter light conditions. Grasses thus fit into contemporary small-space gardens.

Because of its diminutive size, today's smaller garden uses large grasses and other perennials to augment and manipulate space. Because it isn't possible to add actual square footage to the garden, additional space is suggested by the way both paved and planted areas are arranged. What cannot be taken in at a single glance cannot be understood immediately. For example, paving and garden that are not laid out at right angles to property lines but rather as circular or diagonal shapes make space more difficult to comprehend and categorize. Arranging the garden in a way that is not immediately understood makes it seem more spacious.

> *The eye can be easily fooled. Things can be made to seem longer or wider than they really are. This is a great aid, for we can make a small lot seem bigger and so create spaciousness, without increasing garden maintenance and real estate taxes.*
>
> —Thomas Church

A garden is extended in the viewer's mind when space is organized seductively, in an arrangement that leads its viewers into what seem to be far and mysterious reaches of garden. Depth is created by a layering of space and by including very large elements—terraces, stairs, trees, large grasses—within the garden. These add apparent space to the garden; it appears larger, more complicated, and more interesting.

> *Having partially concealed spaces—like a river that moves out of view—is one (element) that may be incorporated into design at any scale. . . . Seductive spaces . . . make us want to move through them.*
>
> —Darrel Morrison

Creating depth by layering, using artist's perspective in which a prominent foreground suggests a deeper background, is another time-honored method of enlarging space. A path or steps that lead into even the smallest garden indicate there is more to be seen. A doorway or trellis adds mystery. Richness of experience enlarges even the tiniest garden.

Large elements in small spaces also suggest roominess. A very large terrace in a small yard makes it seem bigger, especially if it is surrounded by seemingly deep layers of garden. Using giant plants, plants with presence, works to magnify the garden just as the reverse, lining up various small plants along the garden's edges, makes it seem insignificant. Big plants share their proportions and their air of importance with the gardens they inhabit. They are tokens of nature's grandeur and generosity that relate to the sky.

> *A paradoxical magnification of space is effected through the use of tall, sculptural ornamentals. Oversized elements in restricted areas enlarge rather than minimize.*
>
> —James van Sweden

> *Large plants act as focal points. Vision has to be channeled, directed by plants.*
>
> —Wolfgang Oehme

Large, spectacular plants—plants with presence—stop the eye or lead it in the desired direction. They function as the framework for garden tableaux. When they are herbaceous perennials, their growth cycles provide drama and excitement in the garden.

In the new garden, large plants emerge from a matrix of high ground cover. What this ground cover is composed of depends upon climate and taste. Except in cases where the owner is also a dedicated gardener, ground cover should be restricted to only a few plants grown in large masses. Not only does massing simplify maintenance, it bridges the gap between the multicolored perennial border effect and the more tailored look appropriate to landscaping. Perennials used en masse are a happy mixture of gardening and landscaping. The hardest part is choosing which few will serve in an individual garden.

> *Only a little, indeed, of beauty that concerns us most—that of the landscape—can be seized for us.*
>
> —William Robinson

> *The more I plant and the more plantings I plan for the more inclined I grow to restrict the range of material to be used in any one place . . . I know that the most striking and satisfying visual pleasure comes from the repetition or the massing of one simple element.*
>
> —Russell Page

> *When I begin a garden, I think of Mies van der Rohe saying, "Minus is more."*
> —Roberto Burle Marx

Because only a very few plants are used in great numbers, extreme care must be taken to choose only the best—plants with references, proven records of high performance. Karl Foerster said, "The Good jeopardizes the Better." Being satisfied with what is merely good hinders the search for what is better. In addition to being carefully fitted into cultural niches, plants used in the new garden are expected to be the best of the best. Only then can the combination of good looks and low upkeep succeed.

> *A garden with plants that cannot stand the . . . winter weather and have to be protected in all sorts of grotesque ways has lost its poetry and charm.*
> —Jens Jensen

Of course, regional factors enhance or inhibit plant performance. Bananas, which grow rampantly in New Orleans, are a fussy tub plant in Washington, D.C. Paper birches, native north of Pennsylvania, succumb to insect attack farther south; there, the River birch (*Betula nigra*) is a better candidate. Pampas grass, which performs well in zones 8 through 10, should be substituted by ravenna grass in more northerly locations. However, many truly excellent perennials have the right stuff to grow almost anywhere in the country. Among these are daylilies, hemerocallis, coreopsis and black-eyed Susans, *Rudbeckia fulgida* 'Goldsturm.' *Rudbeckia fulgida* 'Goldsturm' makes a good case for the use of

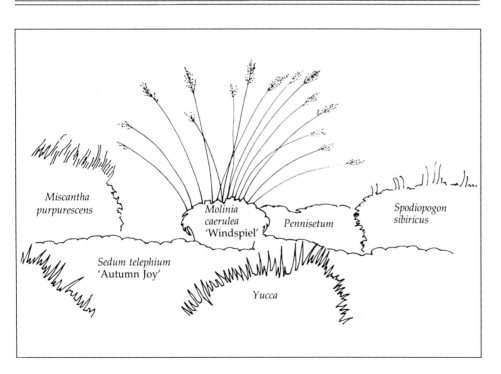

Miscantha
purpurescens

Molinia
caerulea
'Windspiel'

Pennisetum

Spodiopogon
sibiricus

Sedum telephium
'Autumn Joy'

Yucca

Beauty doesn't have to be evergreen. Massing a few outstanding herbaceous plants magnifies seasonal change. Plants with the right stuff are attractive for much of the year. Some turn autumn shapes and colors, making a powerful landscape statement. Dominating a field of luminaries, tall purple moor grass (*Molinia caerulea altissima* 'Windspiel') rises from a river of deep copper 'Autumn Joy' sedums. Behind the molinia is orange *Miscanthus purpurescens*, at left, and winter brown *Spodiopogon sibiricus*, right.

Public landscaping doesn't have to be formal and evergreen. Magnificent ground cover of perennials and grasses at Washington's International Center turns an entire landscape into dynamic garden. Plants emerge, bloom, and wither in rhythm with the seasons. Liberated eyes enjoy the changing show and appreciate the particular beauty of each season. Taken in November, this photograph shows a sweep of achilleas's taupe seed heads, left on the plants all winter, contrasting with the bright green of the perennial plants. Fountain grass (pennisetum) and bright yellow cord grass (spartina) combine with the drab tones of perennials to recall the subtle tones of a country field. *(Design by Oehme, van Sweden & Associates)*

Latin names in selecting plants. Using the common name, "black-eyed Susan," might procure one of a dozen annual or perennial plants with a short period of bloom. 'Goldsturm,' however, is a true perennial, famed for its long-lasting good looks. Another plant with the right stuff is *Sedum telephium* 'Autumn Joy.' From the first emerging rosettes in early spring to the dried bronze flower heads persisting throughout winter, *Sedum telephium* 'Autumn Joy' presents a constantly changing, always attractive garden spectacle completely unlike that of other sedums. Alan Bloom, the great British plantsman, said of 'Autumn Joy,' "This is one of the finest plants ever introduced."

When excellent plants are massed together as magnificent ground cover, the entire landscape becomes garden. When massed, all stages of the plants' growth make powerful statements. Multiplied by a dozen or a hundred, the simple emergence and development of a single plant becomes a grand show, a statement in landscape of the progress of the seasons. The massing of plants enlarges the phenomenon of growth to a scale appropriate and effective for landscape use. The result is a grand chronicle of the seasons, played out in one's own front yard.

Excitement in an ever-changing scene is a vital quality of the new garden. Unfolding over the seasons within this garden is the drama of life itself—the cycle of emergence, growth, fullness, fading, and the long and expectant stillness of winter. In striking contrast, old-style green-on-green landscaping insulates gardens from the vicissitudes of climate, weather, age. Clipped evergreens and irrigated lawns produce a perfectly controlled, artificial landscape that is neat, safe, static, wasteful, and, worst of all, aesthetically dull.

The new American garden ties itself to the natural world around it. The awe one feels for the majesty of nature is generated on a small scale in one's own backyard. Instead of demanding only primary colors, the sophisticated gardener has educated his eye to appreciate the subtle shades of the natural landscape. When the natural world serves as a model, the old reluctance to deal with death and dying—or anything not actively blooming or evergreen—gives way to an acceptance of all phases of the plants' life cycles. Over the garden wall, the falling leaves, the golden grasses of the dry or winter season, and the leafless outlines of trees offer irrefutable proof that beauty isn't evergreen.

> *The world of naturally evolved landscape is a good model to do a better job of the designed landscape. . . . The best design is that which doesn't look designed but looks as if it belongs.*
>
> —Darrel Morrison

A good garden is one composed of suitable plantings. An imitation tropical rain forest in Arizona would not only be wasteful but would reek of kitsch. Less obvious because most Americans have come to expect it everywhere, but equally out of place, a vast lawn that requires constant irrigation is at odds with its environment. A garden that is in

Once this cool, green garden was a square of unhealthy lawn fronting a busy road. Grass required both regular liming and mowing on a difficult slope. Using fallen leaves and branches, the gardener gradually "smothered" lawn and added shade and acid-loving ferns and hostas as ground cover and a hedge of evergreens to screen the road. Maintenance, now limited to transplanting volunteers and pulling out the odd weed, diminishes yearly. Mosses, bloodroot, blue-eyed grass, Jack-in-the-pulpit, and dogwoods volunteer to restore mystery and spontaneity to the garden.

keeping with the spirit of the landscape around it, with vegetation suitable to its locale, a life cycle in tune with surroundings and topographical forms, is beautiful. One at odds with the environment wears the uneasy, unconvincing air of a stage set.

Rightness and suitability of plants and garden to environment allow the garden a life of its own. Guided by nature it is more awesome, more exquisitely beautiful than anything wrought by man. Working with and not against the characteristics of a given site also ensures easier maintenance. Plants do not have to be mollycoddled but thrive in the existing conditions. An even greater plus is the reestablishment of a community of plants so well adapted to site that it naturalizes and begins its own independent progression.

Horticulturists and very experienced gardeners often speak of the concept of "passive gardening," allowing the plants to lead the way and intervening only gently to guide development. Years of experience have taught these gardeners the futility of fighting natural processes. Rather, they cooperate with Nature and let her do much of the work of gardening for them. This means, however, that Nature makes many of the decisions. The garden is no longer the sole expression of its owner but instead a cooperative effort involving gardener, seasons, and conditions of the site.

> *I like a garden in which the plants go it their own way, a garden that is unruly, disorderly, boisterous, even far better than one that is meticulously laid out and cared for. . . . Plants know what they're doing, as your liver and your pancreas know what they're doing, without your interference.*
>
> —Hortense Miller

> *Sometimes wild plants will come in the stonework and come just right, or seeds of garden plants will find lodgment in a crack or joint of masonry and provide some new attractive feature that had never been thought of.*
>
> —Gertrude Jekyll

> *A wood left undisturbed will sustain its character for years and years. . . . Why plant exotic trees that will disturb the natural character of a region and possibly be unsuited to the climate and soil? . . . [Natural] landscape will grow more mellow and stronger as it ages, solving the problems of maintaining a garden while recreating the existing natural look that is now treasured in the mechanized society of today.*
>
> —A. E. Bye

By learning to work with nature, gardeners free themselves from drudgery. When the constant intervention of the hand of man is no longer necessary, spontaneity returns. When the gardener loosens the reins of control, the garden becomes a place of discovery. And when the garden takes on a life of its own—because it is perfectly suited to site—it regains the ability to awe, surprise, and impress. It ceases only to take, to demand in terms of time and labor, and begins to restore the wonder, the peace, and the beauty of the natural world.

Plant Sources

Bog Plants and Waterlilies

Water Ways
10140 Gary Rd.
Potomac, MD 20854
SASE for list

Drought Tolerant Plant Seed

Plants of the Southwest
1812 Second St.
Santa Fe, NM 87501
Plants sold locally; catalog $1

Southwestern Native Seeds
Box 50503
Tucson, AZ 85703
Catalog $1

Hardy Cacti and Succulents

The Cactus Patch
P.O. Box 71
Radium, KS 67571
List 25¢

Perennials and Bulbs

Carroll Gardens
P.O. Box 10
Westminster, MD 21157
Catalog $2

Park's
Cokebury Rd.
Greenwood, SC 29647-0001

Van Bourgondian Bros.
245 Farmingdale Rd., Rt. 109
P.O. Box A
Babylon, NY 11702

Wayside Gardens
Hodges, SC 29695-0001

Prairie Seed

Prairie Seed Source
Box 83
North Lake, WI 53064-0083

Stock Seed Farms
R.R. 1, Box 112
Murdock, NE 68407
Free catalog

Wild Flower/Meadow Mixes

Applewood Seed Company
P.O. Box 10761, Edgemont Station
Golden, CO 80401

Clyde Robin Seed Company
P.O. Box 2366
Castro Valley, CA 94546

Native Plants

Woodlanders, Inc.
1128 Colleton Ave.
Aiken, SC 29801
Trees, shrubs, wild flowers

Sunlight Gardens
Rt. 3, Box 286-B
Loudon, TN 37774
Wild flowers; catalog $1

Ornamental Grasses

Kurt Blumel, Inc.
2543 Hess Rd.
Fallston, MD 21047
Catalog $1

Limerock Ornamental Grasses
R.D. 1, Box 111-C
Port Matilda, PA 16870

Andre Viette Farm and Nursery
State Route 608
Route 1, Box 16
Fisherville, VA 22939
Catalog $2

Bibliography

Bartram, William. *Travels of William Bartram.* Edited by Mark van Doren. New York: Dover Publications, 1955.

Brooks, John. *The Well-Chosen Garden.* New York: Harper & Row, 1984.

Bye, A. E. *Art into Landscape/Landscape into Art.* Mesa, Ariz.: PDA Publishers, 1983.

Church, Thomas. *Your Private World: A Study of Intimate Gardens.* San Francisco: Chronicle Books, 1965.

Church, Thomas, with Grace Hall and Michael Laurie. *Gardens Are for People.* 2d ed. New York: McGraw-Hill, 1983.

Clifford, Joan. *Capability Brown: An Illustrated Life of Capability Brown 1716–1783.* 4th ed. U.K.: Shire Publications, n.d.

Creasy, Rosalind. *Earthly Delights.* San Francisco: Sierra Club Books, 1985.

Downing, Andrew Jackson. *The Architecture of Country Houses.* Reprint. New York: Da Capo Press, 1968.

Eaton, Leonard. *Landscape Artist in America: The Life and Work of Jens Jensen.* Chicago: University of Chicago Press, 1964.

Eckbo, Garrett. *Landscape for Living.* F. W. Dodge, 1950.

Foerster, Karl. *Einzug der Graeser und Farne.* 4th ed. Berlin: Verlag J. Neumann-Neudamm, 1978.

"Friends of the Hortense Miller Garden Newsletter," vol. IX, no. 3, July 1986. Laguna Beach, Calif.

Grounds, Roger. *Ornamental Grasses.* New York: Van Nostrand Reinhold, 1979.

Jensen, Jens. *The Clearing: "A way of life."* Chicago: R. F. Seymour, 1949.

Johnson, Leonard H. *Foundation Planting.* New York: De La Mare, 1927.

Leighton, Ann. *American Gardens in the Eighteenth Century "For Use or Delight."* Boston: Houghton Mifflin, 1976.

Masson, Georgina. *Dumbarton Oaks: A Guide to the Gardens.* Washington, D.C.: Dumbarton Oaks Trustees for Harvard University, 1968.

Newton, Norman T. *Design on the Land.* Cambridge, Mass.: Belknap Press, 1971.

Page, Russell. *Education of a Gardener.* London: Collins, 1971.

Ryan, Deborah E. "The Garden in the Desert." Thesis, Harvard University Graduate School of Design, September, 1982.

Simonds, John Ormsbee. *Landscape Architecture: The Shaping of Man's Natural Environment.* New York: McGraw-Hill, 1961.

Taylor, Christopher. *The Archaeology of Gardens.* U.K.: Shire Archaeology, 1983.

Tice, Patricia M. *Gardening in America, 1830–1910.* Rochester, N.Y.: The Strong Museum, 1984.

Waugh, Frank Albert. *The Natural Style in Landscape Gardening.* Boston: R. G. Badger, 1917.

Wyman, Donald. *Shrubs and Vines for American Gardens.* 3d ed. New York: Macmillan, 1973.

Index